STUDIES IN ENGLISH LITERATURE

Volume LVIII

BLAMETH NAT ME

A Study of Imagery
in Chaucer's Fabliaux

by

JANETTE RICHARDSON
University of California, Berkeley

1970
MOUTON
THE HAGUE · PARIS

Printed in The Netherlands by Mouton & Co., Printers, The Hague.

FOREWORD

A recent spate of publications dealing with rhetoric in both its historical perspectives and its modern possibilities indicates a revival of interest in this the oldest, or very nearly the oldest, intellectual discipline of the Western world. Whereas J. M. Manly could, some forty years ago, speak of Chaucer's artistic development as a process of release from the artificialities of a stultifying rhetoric to "methods of composition based upon close observation of life and the exercise of the creative imagination" (Wharton Lecture on English Poetry, 1926), few contemporary Chaucerians would accept either the accuracy or the implications of such an assertion. Although one still occasionally encounters the words "rhetoric" and "rhetorical" used in a pejorative sense to designate the artificial or the bombastic, most writers today seem to be returning to a more positive recognition of the possibilities of this ancient art and to a reaffirmation of the truth which Longinus long ago asserted – namely, that the best rhetoric is art which conceals art, art which achieves a desired effect without making the reader or listener aware of its mechanics.

It seems to me, however, that not all critics who have concerned themselves with the relation of rhetorical techniques to specific literary works have attained the insight of Longinus. Too frequently they have been content to demonstrate the existence of rhetorical formulae in various specific works rather than to accept the real challenge of rhetorical artistry. They have too often failed to discover how an author transforms the conventional patterns so that they do not appear to be rhetorical devices at all but intimate portions of the organic whole of the given work, and thereby, to illuminate the work of art itself as well as the artistry of its composition. James J. Murphy has recently asserted that we need to "take a new look" at Chaucer and the "rhetoricians" (*RES,* XV (1964), 1-20): perhaps the most profitable application of this injunction would be in terms of such analyses.

The present study attempts, at least, to suggest the mode of approach to Chaucer's use of rhetoric which I believe to be neglected, and although I have limited the topic here to imagery and to a few selected works, I trust that I have accepted the challenge described above. My indebtedness to a host of Chaucerians, past and present, is amply proclaimed by the notes which accompany the text. I wish to extend particular thanks, however, to Professors Bertrand H. Bronson, James M. Cline, Wayne Shumaker, Alain Renoir, and Charles Witke for the criticisms and encouragements which they have given me at various stages in the preparation of this work. I am equally grateful to the University of California for a faculty fellowship grant which aided my progress and to the editors of *English Miscellany* and *ELH* for permission to reprint portions of my original articles on the *Friar's Tale* and the *Shipman's Tale* respectively.[1]

J. R.

[1] "Hunter and Prey", *English Miscellany,* The British Council, XII (1961), 9-20; "The Façade of Bawdry", *ELH,* The Johns Hopkins Press, XXXII (1965), 303-13.

TABLE OF CONTENTS

IMAGERY: MODERN INTEREST AND MEDIEVAL DOCTRINE

I

CHAUCER AND THE MODERN
INTEREST IN IMAGERY

For literary critics of the twentieth century, both theorists and applicative interpreters, imagery as an element of poetic composition has assumed an unprecedented importance. Indeed, the term itself has accumulated so wide a range of meanings that the modern critic is almost forced to specify his own definition when he uses the word, and a host of modifying phrases have of necessity been introduced into contemporary critical jargon: tied imagery, free imagery, static imagery, kinetic imagery, kinaesthetic imagery, synaesthetic imagery, image-cluster, thematic imagery, controlling image, etc. Two basic concepts of the term, however, seem to run throughout the various discussions.[1] Correlated with psychology, imagery may be regarded as any concrete representation by which the poet evokes a mental reproduction of sensations previously experienced by his reader as well as himself. "For every possible kind of sensation there is a corresponding possible image", says I. A. Richards.[2] Correlated with a less physical interpretation of the genesis of thought, imagery may be regarded as a presentation which merges by analogy or comparison separate entities into a single apprehension. Within this concept lie not only the traditional figures of speech but also

---

[1] See, for example: C. Day Lewis, *The Poetic Image* (New York, 1948); Stephen J. Brown, *The World of Imagery* (London, 1927); I. A. Richards, *The Philosophy of Rhetoric* (London, 1936), and *Principles of Literary Criticism* (London, 1924); J. M. Murray, "Metaphor", *Countries of the Mind*, 2nd series (London, 1931); René Wellek and Austin Warren, *Theory of Literature* (New York, 1942); T. E. Hulme, *Speculations* (New York, 1924).

[2] Richards, *Principles*, pp. 121-2.

Ezra Pound's ideographic method[3] and T. S. Eliot's "amalgamation of disparate experience" which is "a direct sensuous apprehension of thought or a recreation of thought into feeling".[4]

The literary theorist's traditional concern with the essence of poetic effect, with analyzing the appeal of poetry to mankind, has also been expressed in terms of these two concepts of imagery. For I. A. Richards, the reader's response is a complex but basic reaction of the nervous system:

Too much importance has always been attached to the sensory qualities of images. What gives an image efficacy is less its vividness as an image than its character as a mental event peculiarly connected with sensation. It is, in a way which no one yet knows how to explain, a relict of sensation and our intellectual and emotional response to it depends far more upon its being, through this fact, a representative of a sensation, than upon its sensory resemblance to one . . . . In other words, what matters is not the sensory *resemblance* of an image to the sensation which is its prototype, but some other relation, at present hidden from us in the jungles of neurology.[5]

Of imagery as comparison, on the other hand, John Middleton Murry asserts:

Metaphor appears as the instinctive and necessary act of the mind exploring reality and ordering experience. It is the means by which the less familiar is assimilated to the more familiar, the unknown to the known . . . . The metaphors of . . . creative literature . . . are the records of an exploration of reality by men who stood head and shoulders above their fellows, who discerned resemblances between the unknown and the known which the generality could not accept nor common speech assimilate.[6]

Applied criticism of this century has perhaps been even more concerned with imagery in all its various senses than has theoretical criticism. The close analysis of literary texts advocated by the so-called New Critics to determine the meaning and value within the work of art itself has inevitably stressed the function of poetic imagery, and the resultant critical explications of works

---

[3] Ezra Pound, *Instigations* (New York, 1920), pp. 357-88.
[4] T. S. Eliot, *Selected Essays, 1917-1932* (New York, 1932), pp. 243-9.
[5] Richards, *Principles*, pp. 119-20.
[6] Murry (note 1), p. 2.

so examined have undeniably enriched the appreciation of the literate world for a wide variety of creative writers. Moreover, since the publication some thirty years ago of Caroline Spurgeon's book on Shakespeare's imagery,[7] a wide-spread interest in possible peripheral applications of the analysis of poetic imagery has developed among literary scholars, some of whom are in no sense critics. As was true with Miss Spurgeon, most investigations of this latter sort have regarded imagery primarily as figurative language.

Even though the results of both critical and scholarly study of imagery have amply demonstrated their value in many different ways, almost all of the attention along these lines has so far been limited to writers of the Elizabethan age and their successors. The work which has been done on Shakespeare, for example, has illuminated the development of his poetic imagination, afforded insights into the workings of his mind, offered supporting evidence for verifying the dating of his plays and the authorship of questionable passages, brought to light previously unrecognized sources for some of his works, and suggested much about his likes and dislikes, his interests, and his experiences (if such conclusions from dramatic imagery are indeed valid). Furthermore – and this is surely the crucial contribution in terms of literary criticism – it has enhanced the appreciation of Shakespeare's artistry by analysis of the ways in which the imagery functions within some of the plays to produce effects to which the reader unconsciously responds without necessarily being aware of the source of his reactions.[8] The poetry of Chaucer has generally failed to attract this kind of study. Such a lacuna in relationship to one of the unchallenged masters of English poetry may, on

---

[7] Caroline Spurgeon, *Shakespeare's Imagery and What It Tells Us* (Cambridge, 1935).

[8] In addition to Spurgeon (note 7), see: Edward A. Armstrong, *Shakespeare's Imagination* (London, 1946); Wolfgang Clemen, *The Development of Shakespeare's Imagery* (Cambridge, 1951); John Erskine Hankins, *Shakespeare's Derived Imagery* (Lawrence, 1953); Robert B. Heilman, *This Great Stage* (Baton Rouge, 1948); G. Wilson Knight, *The Wheel of Fire* (London, 1930), *The Shakespearean Tempest* (London, 1932), *The Imperial Theme* (London, 1939), *The Crown of Life* (London, 1947); Donald A. Stauffer, *Shakespeare's World of Images* (New York, 1949).

first thought, seem strange, yet it is certainly not inexplicable. Narrative poetry in general has proved less tractable than lyric to the new-critical type of analysis; moreover, when compared with the lush abundance of figurative language typical of Elizabethan and many post-Elizabethan poets, Chaucer's imagery seems sparse and simple, and his formal comparisons often merely conventional and decorative. Yet, if imagery is so basic to poetic composition as modern critics have insisted, and if the modern aesthetic axiom that "form and content are inseparable" is indeed true, then surely something valuable can be discovered through examination of Chaucer's practices with imagery, however much his style may differ from that of modern poets.

Chaucerian scholars have not disregarded imagery completely, of course, but their interest has been oblique in so far as they have rarely concerned themselves with the intrinsic meaning and function of imagery within specific works.[9] A few typical com-

---

[9] At the present time the only major study of Chaucer's imagery is Friedrich Klaeber's *Das Bild bei Chaucer* (Berlin, 1893), a work of compilation rather than of interpretation. Klaeber lists all of Chaucer's metaphors and similies, classifies them according to subject matter, and in some cases suggests possible literary sources or points out later uses of the comparisons. Because he separates the figures of speech from their contexts and comments only upon their most obvious surface meanings without reference to their specific use, his work is essentially a specialized concordance.

Several Chaucerians have turned their attention to the imagery of the various spring-time prologues, particularly the first eighteen lines of the *Canterbury Tales*, and have demonstrated the conventionality of the devices and their relationship to the French *reverdie*. See, for example: Arthur W. Hoffman, "Chaucer's Prologue to Pilgrimage: The Two Voices", *English Literary History*, XXI (1954), 1-4; John F. Danby, "Eighteen Lines of Chaucer's 'Prologue' ", *Critical Quarterly*, II (1960), 28-32; Ralph Baldwin, "The Unity of the Canterbury Tales", *Anglistica*, V (Copenhagen, 1955), 20-28.

A few relatively recent studies consider Chaucer's imagery exclusively, but not in a manner which reveals its organic relationship to the effect and meaning of the whole. Elizabeth Rudisill Homann's unpublished doctoral dissertation, "Kinesthetic Imagery in Chaucer" (University of California, Berkeley, 1948), investigates Chaucer's kinaesthetic imagery in terms of both significant gesture and the pacing of movement within some of the narratives; and William A. Tornwall's unpublished doctoral dissertation, "Studies in Chaucer's Imagery" (Louisiana State University, Baton Rouge, 1956), discusses the appropriateness of the subject matter incorporated into

ments from the general critical works on Chaucer's poetry which have been produced in this century may serve as illustration. John Livingston Lowes, for example, notes that the garden in the *Parliament of Fowls* is fabricated from a "blended imagery to which Chaucer and Boccaccio and the Apocalypse and Dante are joint contributors".[10] John Speirs asserts that similes, not metaphors, are characteristic of Chaucer and that "they lucidly promote the visualization essential to allegorical vision", which he believes is the basis of the poet's work.[11] Raymond Preston comments on Chaucer's "reticence" with imagery in the *Troilus* and remarks that he "excels Boccaccio by admitting light and air into the stuffiness of the Italian . . . imagery".[12] J. M. Manly maintains that "imagery, as Chaucer uses it, is a form of diction" and that "his images are not for merely decorative purposes, but because they are needed to convey to the reader the idea that lay in Chaucer's mind in the exact form in which he conceived and felt it".[13] None of these Chaucerians, nor indeed, with a few exceptions,[14] any other, exhibits a direct interest in imagery as it

---

Chaucer's metaphors and similes and examines the poet's treatment of derived images. In addition, R. K. Gordon, "Chaucer's Imagery", *Transactions of the Royal Society of Canada*, XXXIII, ser. 3, sec. 2 (1939), 81-90, follows the lead of Caroline Spurgeon in attempting to show how Chaucer's figures of speech throw light upon his tastes, his preferences, and the life of his times; and Paull F. Baum, "Chaucer's Nautical Metaphors", *South Atlantic Quarterly*, XLIX (1950), 67-73, comments upon the nautical metaphors in the *Troilus* and concludes that Chaucer drew his images not from the sea but from the ending of the *Filostrato*.

[10]   John Livingstone Lowes, *Geoffrey Chaucer* (Boston, 1934), pp. 149-50.
[11]   John Speirs, *Chaucer the Maker* (London, 1951), p. 25.
[12]   Raymond, Preston, *Chaucer* (London, 1952), pp. 58-9.
[13]   John Matthews Manly, *Some New Light on Chaucer* (New York, 1926), p. 284.
[14]   Three names must certainly be mentioned as exceptions. At the English Institute in 1950, Sanford B. Meech read a paper – since reproduced in his book *Design in Chaucer's Troilus* (Syracuse, 1959) – on "figurative contrasts" in *Troilus and Criseyde*. Comparing Chaucer's poem with Boccaccio's *Filostrato*, Mr. Meech demonstrates how the use of certain image clusters supports the complexity of Chaucer's characterizations and emphasizes contrasts between the hero and the other major figures, Criseyde, Pandarus, and Diomede. Charles Muscatine, "Form, Texture and Meaning in Chaucer's *Knight's Tale*", *PMLA*, LXV (1950), 911-29, suggests a thematic use of imagery in the first of the *Canterbury Tales* and argues

functions organically within the aesthetic whole of an individual narrative.

Yet, curiously enough, although Chaucer may be "reticent" with imagery, although his metaphors and similes ARE simple and "lucid" in their surface application, although his comparisons are often commonplace or conventional if not actually borrowed, he frequently manipulates this imagery so that it produces or reinforces effects relevant to the aesthetic whole of a specific poem rather than merely affording a single impression fitting only to the immediate line or passage. Indeed, as this study will attempt to demonstrate, in much of his later work which is dominated by comic irony, including all of his fabliaux, he seems to have developed a distinctive technique for utilizing imagery so that it interacts ironically with other elements of a narrative to perform an organic, unifying function. As with Shakespeare, so with Chaucer, although the method is vastly different – imagery operates to produce effects to which the reader (or audience, if you prefer) unconsciously responds, albeit he rarely realizes from what source his reaction stems.

The term "imagery" as used in the ensuing discussion refers both to those impressions evoked by description and to formal figures of speech; the designation is essentially that of C. Day Lewis, who says: "an epithet, a metaphor, a simile may create an image; or an image may be presented to us in a phrase or passage on the face of it purely descriptive, but conveying to our imagination something more than the accurate reflection of an external

---

that the elaborate descriptions and the "sub-surface" images of disorder all reinforce what he calls the "heart of the poem's meaning as well as its structure": the conservative concept of order as embodied in the "design of the noble life". Mr. Muscatine, like many modern critics, regards imagery in its broadest terms as any kind of sensory impression, and his later book, *Chaucer and the French Tradition* (Los Angeles and Berkeley, 1957), contains some pertinent references to such imagery in several of the *Canterbury Tales*, although this interest is only a minor facet of his concept of conventional, naturalistic, and mixed styles. Most provocative is Charles A. Owen, "The Crucial Passages in Five of the Canterbury Tales: A Study in Irony and Symbol", *JEGP*, LII (1953), 294-311, although his analysis is limited to such imagery as appears in his five selected passages.

reality".[15] Although this definition is more limited than the concept used by many modern critics, it may be appropriately applied to Chaucer's art; for inasmuch as he was influenced by medieval rhetorical-poetic doctrines,[16] his own idea of poetic imagery, had he been aware of the term, would be precisely this. The writers on poetic theory and practice included description and figures of speech in the formulae for poetic decoration and offered suggestions for their use under such classifications as "descriptive dilation" and the figures of *demonstratio, effictio, imago, similitudo,* and *translatio.* A figure of speech or a passage of description was, therefore, a recognized poetic device, a defined segment of a poet's artistry, to be employed with careful deliberation. Because Chaucer's peculiar technique with imagery seems necessarily to result from conscious manipulation, it is desireable to discuss his practice in terms of such devices as he would have considered part of his craft.

[15] Day Lewis (note 1), p. 18.

[16] Since the publication in 1924 of Edmond Faral's edition of the major thirteenth-century treatises on poetics, a number of scholars have been concerned with Chaucer's use of traditional rhetorical devices, among which are various figures which produce what we would now consider imagery. Of these, Chaucer's handling of the portrait, or *effictio,* has been most thoroughly investigated, both for its conventional aspects and for the poet's innovations. In general, these studies emphasize the relationship of Chaucer's practices to the rhetorical formulae rather than analyzing his use of rhetorical devices as part of an aesthetic whole. See, for example: John Matthews Manly, *Chaucer and the Rhetoricians,* Warton Lecture on English Poetry, 17 (Milford, 1926); Traugott Naunin, *Der Einfluss der mittelalterlichen Rhetorik auf Chaucers Dichtung* (Bonn, 1929); Karl Young, "Chaucer and Geoffrey of Vinsauf", *Modern Philology,* XLI (1944), 172-82; Marie Padgett Hamilton, "Notes on Chaucer and the Rhetoricians", *PMLA,* XLVII (1932), 403-9; Benjamin S. Harrison, "Medieval Rhetoric in the *Book of the Duchess*", *PMLA,* XLIX (1934), 428-42; and Dorothy Everett, "Some Reflections on Chaucer's 'Art Poetical' ", in *Essays on Middle English Literature* (Oxford, 1955). For a recent re-evaluation of Chaucer's relationship to the medieval rhetoricians, see: Robert O. Payne, *The Key of Remembrance: A Study of Chaucer's Poetics* (New Haven, 1963).

II

THE MEDIEVAL CONCEPT OF IMAGERY

The concept of imagery with all of the possible ramifications suggested in the previous chapter is essentially an invention of the twentieth century. Chaucer, in fact, would not even have known the word, much less its modern complexities. In the critical vocabulary of the late Middle Ages, the term *imago* designated a specific figure of comparison closely related to the modern simile although not defined with the same precision. However, because poets from time immemorial have made descriptive and figurative language an intrinsic part of their art, such poetic theory as Chaucer could have known did not fail to consider, in some measure, various specific devices which critics now incorporate into the generic term "imagery". If Chaucer's technique with imagery is to be properly evaluated in its historical context,[1] the nature of medieval theory as it relates to imagery must first be examined.

The categorizing treatises on poetics which were written during

[1] In his recent book, *A Preface to Chaucer: Studies in Medieval Perspectives* (Princeton, 1962), D. W. Robertson, Jr. has protested vigorously that modern critical methods cannot be applied to Chaucer's poetry; it can be understood correctly, he asserts, only if it is viewed in its historical context, which he prescribes primarily as its relationship to the Christian scriptural and exegetical tradition. The demand which this highly controversial book makes for an adequate historical perspective is surely valid, even though Professor Robertson's own critical method has been seriously questioned. Yet, perhaps equally valid is the modern concept that a work of art contains within itself its aesthetic totality; and if so, Chaucer's poetry, like any other, can be profitably subjected to close analysis which reveals the components of its artistry. Indeed, I see no reason why historical perspective and artistic analysis should be considered mutually exclusive.

the high Middle Ages, and which are particularly relevant to any analysis of Chaucer's art, were all rhetorical in orientation; and their authors – Matthew of Vendôme, Geoffrey of Vinsauf, Eberhard the German, Gervais of Melkley, and John of Garland – are frequently, if erroneously, grouped together as "the medieval rhetoricians". As various scholars have pointed out,[2] the concepts expounded by these writers ultimately derived from the grammatical and rhetorical doctrines which constituted a major portion of classical Roman education. According to J. W. H. Atkins, the "channels through which such teaching reached the Middle Ages were the works of Cicero and Quintilian, imperfectly understood, the rhetorical and grammatical treatises of fourth-century philologians, together with the encyclopaedic works of Capella, Cassiodorus and Isidore."[3] Of particular importance was the anonymous *Rhetorica ad Herennium* (c. 85 B.C.),[4] a text which promulgated Hellenistic instruction on oratory and which the Middle Ages erroneously attributed to Cicero. The medieval theorists, intermingling rhetoric with poetic and distinguishing between the two by the single criterion of whether a work was verse or prose, were largely content to discuss poetry in terms of the figures which had originally been established as useful linguistic patterns for the art of persuasion, be it deliberative, forensic, or epideictic. Matthew of Vendôme, for example, defines poetry in his *Ars Versificatoria* (written before 1175) as: "Versus est metrica oratio succincte." He adds, however, that a mere counting of feet and knowledge of quantities [dinumeratio pedum, cognitio temporum] does not produce poetry; "elegans junctura dictionum" is also necessary, and it is primarily to the techniques of rhetoric that he turns for his materials in teaching this tasteful

[2] See: J. W. H. Atkins, *English Literary Criticism: The Medieval Phase* (Cambridge, 1943); Baldwin, *Medieval Rhetoric and Poetic* (New York, 1928); Edmond Faral, *Les Arts Poétiques du XIIe et XIIIe Siècle* (Paris, 1924).

[3] Atkins (note 2), p. 23. See also Ernst R. Curtius, *European Literature and the Latin Middle Ages*, trans. Willard R. Trask (New York, 1953), pp. 65-76.

[4] Curtius (note 3), p. 66. For a full discussion of the problems of authorship, date, sources, and purpose of the *ad Herennium*, see: Harry Caplan, ed., *Ad C. Herennium*, Loeb Classical Library (Cambridge, 1954), pp. vii-xxxiv.

combining of words.[5] However inadequate this basic assumption
regarding the nature of poetry may now seem, and however
mechanical and excessively schematized the treatises of the
twelfth and thirteenth centuries may be, the approach was not
entirely inconsistent with poetic practice, for the elaborate techniques of rhetoric had indeed been adapted to poetry centuries
before and had become, in the words of E. R. Curtius, "the
common denominator of literature in general".[6]

Of these medieval theorists, Chaucer was familiar with the
work of at least one: Geoffrey of Vinsauf. The apostrophe in the
Nun's Priest's Tale to "Gaufred, deere maister soverayn" (3347),[7]
and the narrator's ironic regret that he has neither the "sentence"
nor the "loore" to chide the Friday of Chaunticleer's downfall as
this "maister" had the Friday of Richard I's death, has long been
recognized [8] as a reference to one of the passages (375 ff.) illustrating the use of the apostrophe which Geoffrey of Vinsauf gives
in his Poetria Nova, written between 1208 and 1213.[9] As has
also been noted, in Troilus and Criseyde Chaucer incorporates a
condensed translation of the beginning of the Poetria Nova (43-
8) to describe Pandarus' reaction to the announcement of love
laboriously extracted from Troilus (I, 1065-9); and several
modern scholars have argued for less overt influences of Geoffrey's text upon the English poet.[10] Whether Chaucer knew any

[5]   Faral (note 2), pp. 110-11. All subsequent quotations from and references to the texts of Matthew of Vendôme, Geoffrey of Vinsauf, and
Eberhard the German are from this edition. Translations are my own, and
emphasis is always supplied. See pp. 3 and 14 for argument that the Ars
Versificatoria should be dated before 1175.
[6]   Curtius, p. 70.
[7]   This and all subsequent quotations (and line numbers) are from
Chaucer's Complete Works, 2nd edition, ed. F. N. Robinson (Cambridge,
1957); emphasis is always supplied.
[8]   The allusion was first identified by John Bale, in the mid-sixteenth century, and was recorded by Speght in his second edition of Chaucer's works
(1602). See: Young, "Chaucer and Geoffrey of Vinsauf", p. 172.
[9]   Faral, pp. 28-33, presents evidence for so dating the poem.
[10]   Hamilton, "Notes on C. and the Rhetoricians", suggests that Pandarus'
advice on letter-writing in Troilus and Criseyde (II. 1028-9) echoes the
Poetria Nova, 1933-5; Henry Barret Hinckley, "Chauceriana", Modern
Philology, XVI (1918), 39, conjectures that Chaucer may have derived his
use of the word "colour" to apply to rhetorical figures from the Poetria

of the rhetorical treatises other than the *Poetria Nova* cannot be asserted positively, but his various references to rhetorical terminology suggest that he was acquainted with the common doctrines which all of the texts propound.[11] His Franklin, obviously

---

Nova; Young (note 8), pp. 172-82, argues that the "moralistic" or "sermonistic" themes in the *Nun's Priest's Tale* may well have been suggested by other examples of the apostrophe in the *Poetria Nova* (the lament for Richard I's death is but one of six such illustrations) and by glosses which are found in many of the MSS; Robert Armstrong Pratt, "The Classical Lamentations in the *Nun's Priest's Tale*", *Modern Language Notes*, LXIV (1949), 76-8, points out that five lines before the lament for Richard I, the *Poetria Nova* mentions Ilion, Carthage, and Rome, and he hypothesizes that Chaucer got the idea for his references to classical lamentations (*N. Priest's T.*, 3335-74) from this passage.

[11] In his Warton lecture, *Chaucer and the Rhetoricians*, p. 96, Manly asserts that "the *Nova Poetria* was one of the principal textbooks on rhetoric and was studied in the schools with a zeal devoted perhaps to few modern school books". Unfortunately, he gives no proof for this statement, and the only verification which I have been able to find is the passage in Eberhard's *Laborintus* which Faral identifies as Geoffrey's *Poetria*:

> Ars nova scribendi speciali fulget honore,
> Rebus cum verbis deliciosa suis.

> (665-6)

Eberhard devotes some ninety lines to mentioning authors which he thinks should be given to students; along with Virgil, Horace, Statius, and many other classical poets, he lists medieval writers, including the grammarian Eberhard of Bethune, Matthew of Vendôme, and Geoffrey of Vinsauf, if these lines do indeed refer to him.

In fact, in spite of the popular notion that rhetoric flourished as one of the branches of the *trivium*, scholarly investigation seems to deny that such was the case in the high Middle Ages. Writing of the English grammar school, Foster Watson states: "There is no evidence of the systematic school-teaching of Rhetoric in the Middle Ages." (*The English Grammar Schools to 1660: their Curriculum and Practice* (Cambridge, 1908), p. 440.) Writing of medieval universities, Louis J. Paetow says: "Deprived almost absolutely of its most important function, that of training for eloquence, rhetoric lost much of its individuality. Its doctrines were often merged with those of grammar; [and it became] at best ... but a branch auxiliary to grammar and dialectic. It is not surprising therefore to find that very little of the old formal medieval rhetoric was taught at the universities. At the end of the twelfth century, it was more popular at Paris than it was to be later when the university was fully developed .... The same was even more true in other French universities. At Toulouse, for example, where a good deal of stress was laid on grammar, not a trace can be found of instruction in old-fashioned rhetoric .... At Bologna and in Italy generally it suffered especially in the thirteenth century ... but

thinking of the *Rhetorica ad Herennium,* disclaims any knowledge of Cicero and the "colours of rethoryk" (*Frank. Pro.,* 718-27); the Squire avows that it would take "a rethor excellent,/ That koude his colours longynge for that art" to describe Canacee's beauty adequately (*Sq. Tale,* 34-41); the Nun's Priest, commenting upon the fact that worldly joy soon passes, asserts that "if a rethor koude faire endite", he might safely record this *sententia* in a chronicle as a "sovereyn notabilitee" (*Nun's P. Tale,* 3207-9); the Host, while urging the Clerk to telle a "pleyn" tale, says:

> Youre termes, youre colours, and youre figures,
> Keepe hem in stoor til so be that ye endite
> Heigh style, as whan that men to kynges write.
> (*Clerk's Pro.,* 16-18)

And the pedantic eagle of *The House of Fame* brags that his verbose explanation of the nature of sound has been presented without any subtlety of speech or great prolixity "Of figures of poetrie/ Or colours of rethorike" (II, 853-64).

Whatever may have been the extent of Chaucer's reading in sources upon which he might base such allusions to rhetorical "colors", it is appropriate for the purposes of the present dis-

---

began to prosper again early in the fourteenth. The establishment of a special chair in rhetoric at Bologna in 1321 has been noted. The information in the statutes is very meagre but we learn that early in the fifteenth century there were distinct examinations and graduations in rhetoric .... There can remain no doubt that the study of formal rhetoric did not flourish at the universities even as much as it had done in the best schools of the early Middle Ages." (*The Arts Course at Medieval Universities with Special Reference to Grammar and Rhetoric, University of Illinois Studies,* III, no. 7 (Urbana, 1910), pp. 67-70.) In his unpublished doctoral dissertation, "Chaucer, Gower and the English Rhetorical Tradition" (Stanford University, 1956), James J. Murphy has investigated this question at length. Upon a variety of substantial evidence, he concludes that although grammar, song, and dialectic were taught as lower-school subjects, "*rhetorica* is not named as a part of the curriculum of any fourteenth-century non-university" English school (p. 111), and that there was "no well-established concept of rhetorical training" at Oxford before 1431 (p. 124).

It is true, of course, that both metrics and figures of speech were incorporated into the study of grammar in the Middle Ages (see: Curtius, pp. 42-5), but that Geoffrey's *Poetria* was either designed for or particularly adaptable to being used as a school text for the grammar curriculum seems highly dubious (see *infra,* pp. 23-25).

cussion to concentrate upon what the *Poetria Nova* offers relevant to imagery, since it is not only the text with which Chaucer acknowledges familiarity,[12] but also the one which seems to have been most widely circulated.[13] It should be noted, however, that Geoffrey's *Poetria* is in many ways far more sophisticated than the analogous treatises. The approach to the subject used by all the authors is pedagogic: they intend to offer instruction to aspiring poets rather than to formulate an abstract theory of poetry.

[12]   Murphy (note 11) argues that Chaucer did not know the *Poetria Nova* in its entirety. He points out that although Faral lists sixteen MSS extant in England, only two of these can with any assurance have been available to Chaucer: the only identifiably English MS is the fragmentary form in the Old Royal Collection at the British Museum, and the Bodleian Library has one fourteenth-century MS which is perhaps English (p. 136). In medieval catalogues he has found only one copy, that listed in the 1391 catalogue of the Durham libraries (pp. 131-3). Although he admits that valid conclusions cannot be drawn from what surviving manuscripts might seem to indicate, he combines this evidence with his conviction that rhetoric was not taught in fourteenth-century schools to decide that Chaucer would not have known Geoffrey's text. He argues that the reference in the *Nun's Priest's Tale* to Geoffrey and his lament for Richard I's death may very well be based upon knowledge of the *planctus* alone, for it was both circulated separately and included in Nicholas Trivet's *Annales* (1328). Since Chaucer used Trivet's *Chronicle* for the tale of Constance, Mr. Murphy alleges that Chaucer very likely knew the *Annales* also. To dispose of the translated passage in the *Troilus*, he argues that the image of the builder is not unique with Geoffrey (however, one notes that Chaucer's passage far more closely parellels lines 43-8 of the *Poetria Nova* than any of the other instances mentioned) and then states that even if the source is the *Poetria*, Chaucer need not have read more than the beginning of the treatise since Geoffrey's figure comes at the first.
  Although Mr. Murphy's scholarship is admirable, one can hardly help questioning his conclusion. Why should Chaucer stop reading the *Poetria* after the first fifty lines? Moreover, even though rhetoric very likely did not figure significantly in the education of the day, Chaucer as a poet would surely have a special interest in a work which discussed his own craft and which he COULD have read, either in England or ON THE CONTINENT, despite the fact that we now have but limited evidence of its existence in fourteenth-century England. Chaucer's own use of rhetoric and of the *Poetria Nova* specifically seems better proof of his knowledge than does Mr. Murphy's reconstruction of a possible lack of such knowledge.
[13]   Baldwin (note 2), p. 187. Faral, pp. 13-14, 27-28, 37, 38-39, cites more than forty extant MSS of the *Poetria Nova* and states that this list is far from complete; for Matthew of Vendôme's *Ars Versificatoria* he lists five, for Eberhard's *Laborintus* fifteen, and for Gervais of Melkley's *Ars Versificaria* three.

Matthew of Vendôme, for example, begins his *Ars Versificatoria* with the assertion that the work is an introduction to poetry which aims at practical usefulness ["ad versuum introductionem praesens spectat negotium" (I. 1)] and concludes with remarks about the respective responsibilities of instructor and student (IV. 32-48), both passages no doubt influencing Faral in his conjecture that the treatise probably emerged from Matthew's teaching in the schools of Orleans.[14] The method of instruction invariably includes definitions of figures descended from what was traditionally the third of five parts in the art of classical rhetoric, *elocutio* or style, although this subject matter had been incorporated into the study of grammar in the Middle Ages; and the authors illustrate the figures mentioned with quotations from classical poets or examples of their own composing. Indeed, the *Summa de Coloribus Rhetoricis,* which is also attributed to Geoffrey, is nothing more than a flat, matter-of-fact handbook which lists, defines, and illustrates twenty-four of the *exornationes verborum* (ornaments of diction) and one of the *exornationes sententiarum* (ornaments of thought) from the *Rhetorica ad Herennium.* Even Eberhard's *Laborintus,* which was written between 1212 and 1280,[15] and which differs from most of its counterparts in its fanciful introduction and its abandonment of prose, adopts a pattern of two lines of definition, two lines of illustration when discussing the traditional figures. Geoffrey's *Poetria,* however, is more pretentious. He too employs the pedagogic tone – for example, he admonishes: "if, in pursuing the path of poetic composition, you wish to be led well, entrust yourself to a sure leader; ponder what is written below" ["si vis bene duci,/ Te certo committe duci; subscripta revolve" (210-11)] – but he devotes relatively little space to definitions, frequently omits naming the devices being discussed, and assumes familiarity with the explanations of figures given in the *ad Herennium* ["quos omnes lege plenius in Cicerone" (1251)]. He dedicates his work to Pope Innocent III and appends an epilogue urging that

---

[14] Faral, p. 14.
[15] *Ibid.,* p. 39. Faral can find no evidence for a more precise dating of the poem.

the Pope be magnaminous and reconcile his disputes with King
John of England:

Pro principe nostro
Supplico. Sum minimus: es maximus; attamen esto
Flexilis, et sit ei melius ratione petentis.   (2096-8)

[I make supplication in behalf of my prince. I am least: you are most
great; yet for all that, be flexible, and may it be the better for him
because of the nature of my petition.]

The political purpose implied by these references suggests that
Geoffrey at least hoped for an audience of the greatest importance, and to this end, he seems to have attempted to create a
work which would both illustrate his own poetic powers and
expound his fullest understanding of the art. Writing in Latin
verse rather than the customary prose, he sets forth his doctrines
in a highly figurative style, often expounding his most important
concepts in metaphor or explaining a figure and commenting
upon its use while simultaneously employing the figure. As the
result of his endeavors to demonstrate his own poetic versatility,
his discussion is often ambiguous, but more than any of his fellow
"rethors", he gives consideration to WHY a poet composes figures
rather than merely explaining HOW he does so. Thus, it is possible
to deduce a fuller theory of imagery from his treatise than from
the others and, by so doing, to delineate a medieval standard
with which Chaucer's technique with imagery can be compared.

Geoffrey organizes his *Poetria* into four major parts, and he
introduces each section with general commentary on the value
and function of the techniques which are about to be explained
and illustrated. His statements pertinent to imagery appear in the
second and third sections of the work, which include his version
of the figures from classical rhetoric, and he entitles these divi-
sions respectively: "cura ... qua compensare statera/ Pondera,
si juste pendet sententia" and "sudor ... ut corpus verborum non
sit agreste,/ Sed civile" (81-4). According to the generally accepted modern belief that Geoffrey's treatise is exclusively concerned with superficial techniques and specious ornamentation,[16]

[16]   See, for example: Atkins, pp. 95-100; Manley, *C. and the Rhet.*, pp.
101-2; 112; Everett, "Reflections on 'Art Poetical' ", p. 151; Charles Sears
Baldwin, "Cicero on Parnassus", *PMLA*, XLII (1927), 110-112.

this second section is merely a mechanical listing of ways for the poet to amplify or abbreviate his verse, primarily the former (for which Geoffrey's modern detractors would like to substitute the pejorative term "to pad"), and the third section is an equally mechanical listing of devices with which the poet can decorate his utterance. However, if one does not allow the sheer bulk of Geoffrey's explanatory and illustrative passages to overshadow what he says in the generalized introductory commentary, it seems that Geoffrey's concepts are somewhat less superficial than modern scholars have agreed that they are. Secure in the oft-repeated judgment that Geoffrey regards the writing of poetry as a purely mechanical process, for example, no one has seen fit to mention the fact that he speaks explicitly in his introduction to section two of the fire of genius [*ignis ingenii*] as a requisite for the true poet. Although he warns that an aspiring poet must labor long and hard at his craft (209-10), he also expresses an awareness that imitation and effort alone will not suffice:

> Formula materiae, quasi quaedam formula cerae,
> Primitus est tactus duri: si sedula cura
> Igniat ingenium, subito mollescit ad ignem
> Ingenii sequiturque manum quocumque vocarit,
> Ductilis ad quicquid.   (213-17)

[The form of poetic material, like the form of wax, is first hard to the touch; but, if diligent care ignite genius, suddenly the form grows soft in the fire of genius and follows the hand whithersoever it shall have designated, malleable into anything.]

Brief as this statement is, Geoffrey at least acknowledges that mechanical endeavor will not suffice without that intangible sensibility variously labelled as talent, inspiration, or genius, even though he does not go so far in this recognition as does Gervais of Melkley, the only other medieval writer on poetics to mention such a concept. Gervais explicitly asserts in his *Ars Versificaria* (?1213-16) [17] that genius surpasses all teaching in poetic art and that often an acute mind ignorant of theory may spontaneously create rhetorical felicities:

---

[17] Faral, pp. 35-7, tentatively dates the work thus.

In hac arte si assit exercitium praecedit ingenium instructorem. Quippe practica rethorice naturali industrie vicinissima occurrit spontanea animo subtili etiam theoricam ignoranti.[18]

Indeed, despite the fact that Gervais is in the process of writing an instructive treatise, he admits that such a work has decided limitations even for those with merely "studiosis animis". He recommends that they should not spend long hours learning theory but should rather devote themselves to perceptive reading [legendo medullitus] of other writers, both ancient and modern, and to composing their own verse. It is true that neither Gervais nor Geoffrey develops this idea extensively, but to ignore their assertions entirely and insist that medieval poetic theory is nothing more than a concept of mechanical dilation by means of colors of rhetoric is to falsify the texts.

In similar fashion, to dismiss most of Geoffrey's entire second section as mere amplification is equally questionable. Certainly the phrase which he chooses as the sub-heading for the section ["cura ... qua compensare statera/ Pondera, si juste pendet sententia"] suggests a deeper insight than simply amplification for the sake of amplification. Using the metaphor of a weighing balance (and perhaps his word "juste" is intended to evoke an image of the scales of Justice), he implies that the value of the thought [sententia] must be equalized by the weight of the expression. Because he allows the metaphor to stand here without further elaboration, it is difficult to determine its precise meaning, but when he later returns to the subject, "weight of expression" [pondera] seems to involve length, or what might be called rhetorical emphasis achieved through the sheer amount of space devoted to developing an idea. He speaks metaphorically of the poet's coming to a place where two roads meet and where he must choose either the broad or the narrow path, or, as he more prosaically states it, must choose either to note a thing briefly or to expand it at length:

---

[18]   Gervais' text is inedited. I am indebted to the curator of manuscripts and the library of the University of Glasgow for providing me with photostats of Hunterian MS. 511 (V.8.14). The emendations (italicized) which I have made in the second sentence are necessary for the sake of meaning. The scribal error in both cases is nothing more than the omission of a macron.

Curritur in bivio: via namque vel ampla vel arta,
Vel fluvius vel rivus erit; vel tractius ibis
Vel cursim salies; vel rem brevitate notabis,
Vel longo sermone trahes.   (206-9)

Geoffrey then proceeds to explain and illustrate eight methods of expanding a thing [rem], without making further reference to his original concept of the purpose of amplification. As soon as he turns from introduction to precept, he ceases to give even the slightest hint that technique is not the end in itself. Although he apparently expects his readers to keep in mind that some relationship should exist between the thought and the use of the devices explained, it is impossible to detect any signs of the idea latent in his definitions, and he obscures the issue completely by providing lavish examples which Horace would surely have considered purple patches. The question which must be answered, of course, is what does Geoffrey mean by "sententia" and by the later completely vague analogous term "rem". Does he intend "sententia" (thought) to represent what would now be called "theme", the central or dominating idea of a literary work? Or does he intend it to convey a suggestion of what the rhetorical figure *sententia* (proverb or maxim) embodies and thus to imply a moral or didactic idea? Or does he use the term simply for the poet's conception of something to say, so that the word "rem" (thing) is an exact equivalent? He does not make this explicit, and it is only when one has read the whole of the *Poetria*, and pondered upon the implications of a number of scattered passages, that the concept which Geoffrey himself fails to set forth with any sort of clarity begins to take on a kind of consistency which he apparently assumes is obvious.

In the third section, which Geoffrey initially categorizes as the toil involved in making the words of a poem civil rather than barbarous ["sudor . . . ut corpus verborum non sit agreste,/ Sed civile" (82-4)], he returns to the concept, introduced nearly seven hundred lines earlier, of the importance of the thought within a poem, but here, as in the second section, his handling of this subject, which he seems to regard as a basic consideration for poetic composition, is inconsistent and unsatisfactory.

In introducing the section, he insists upon a difference between the "interior" and the "exterior" of words and emphatically warns against the "contemptible, sordid" practice of employing words whose internal "color" does not conform to their external:

> Verbi prius inspice mentem
> Et demum faciem, cujus ne crede colori:
> Se nisi conformet color intimus exteriori,
> Sordet ibi ratio: (739-42)

To depict only the surface [faciem] of a word, he says, is to paint a picture of clay; the result is false, a feigned form, a white-washed wall, a hypocritical expression pretending to be something although it is nothing ["se simulans aliquid, cum sit nihil", (745)]. It shows off on the outside but has nothing within ["se jactitat extra,/ Sed nihil intus habet', (746-7)]. Therefore, the poet must examine the words he uses with care and acuteness, for a worthy thought [sententia] must not be disgraced with ignoble word choice. A rich thought must be honored by a rich word, lest a noble matron blush in pauper's rags:

> Sententia si sit honesta,
> Ejus ei servetur honos: ignobile verbum
> Non inhonestet eam, sed, ut omnia lege regantur,
> Dives honoretur sententia divite verbo,
> Ne rubeat matrona potens in paupere panno.
>   (751-55)

The shift in point of emphasis, and indeed in essential meaning, which is evident in this introductory passage typifies the dilemma that Geoffrey is incapable of avoiding in his attempt to correlate matter and method. What he says in the first half of the passage condemns specious ornamentation; yet, as soon as he mentions worthy thoughts, he can discuss their presentation only in terms of fitting adornment. He himself seems completely unaware of the danger of this dual position – a danger amply verified by modern critics' judgment of his work as a document teaching superficial ornamentation. His inability to perceive any inconsistency in recommending on one level what he has just condemned on another allows him to proceed quite contentedly from his climactic image of the aristocrat in pauper's rags to a discussion of rejuvenating the FACES of old words (763-4), even though he has protested painting the FACE of a word only twenty-one lines earlier!

In this third section, in which Geoffrey explains and illustrates the ornaments (i.e. figures) of diction (*exornationes verborum*) and the ornaments of thought (*exornationes sententiarum*) from the *Rhetorica ad Herennium*, he not only protests against the idea of ornamentation but he also, with apparently deliberate intention, avoids the classical terminology which suggests adornment.[19] He labels his passage devoted to the *exornationes sententiarum*, for example, as "flores, quibus est sententia vocum/ Florida" (1230-1) [flowers in which the very thought of the utterance is in bloom], and he repeats this flower image again and again. However, despite his assertions, he continues to confuse his concept of the relationship between thought and expression by further seemingly contradictory praises of adornment.

In the conclusion to his discussion of varieties of metaphor, he urges that the poet be extremely careful in his adapting [transsumere] of words to form metaphors, for this figure easily lends itself to false "exterior" color:

> Tamen esto modestus,
> Ne sis inflatus nec turgidus. Haec duo mixta
> Sunt et honos et onus: onus est transsumere vocem
> Ut decet, est et honos cum sit transsumpta decenter.
> (945-8)

[Nevertheless, be moderate, lest you be swollen or bombastic. In this device both honor and difficulty are mixed: it is a burden to adapt a word as is fitting, but it is an honor when it is adapted fittingly.]

Yet, when he goes on to describe the pleasure given by a metaphor in which the expression is thus appropriately fitted to the sense, he writes:

> Quando venit tali sententia *culta paratu*,
> Ille sonus vocum laetam dulcescit ad aurem.
> Et fricat interius nova delectatio mentem.
> (949-51)

[19] The division indicated in this section between "difficult" and "easy ORNAMENTS" is Faral's editorial addition. He takes his terminology for the two major categories (*ornatus difficilis; ornatus facilis*) from the prose *Documentum* ascribed to Geoffrey.

[When the thought comes adorned with such a fitting out, the very sound of the words becomes sweet to the pleased ear, and it soothes the inner mind with a new delight.]

Thought "adorned" with a "fitting out" which is both moderate and appropriate – this is obviously the goal, and thus his plea for "fitness" [transsumere vocem ut decet], which would appear to be connected with his earlier concern for equating the value of a thought with the weight of its expression, leads to a pleasing, immediate, surface appropriateness of language to convey the "sententia".

From these and other passages, it becomes evident that Geoffrey regards form and content as basically separate elements in poetry, a concept which contemporary literary theorists have vehemently denied. Later in the *Poetria*, Geoffrey warns the poet to avoid obscurity in his use of those figures which are commonly called tropes. These devices should serve as a key to unlock the mind. If a figure merely clouds the thought, it fails in its purpose; the poet makes a lock out of what should be the key:

> Quae clausum reserent animum sunt verba reperta,
> Ut quaedam claves animi: qui vult aperire
> Rem clausam, nolit verbis inducere nubem;
> Si tamen induxit, facta est injuria verbis:
> Fecit enim de clave seram.   (1065-69)

Thus, the manner of expression is not something which subtly shapes the content; it either succeeds in conveying the poet's thought clearly or it draws a cloud over the idea. The manner of expression, however, does (or should) provide a pleasing and appropriate garb for the content. Geoffrey's final statement on the use of all the figures discussed in the third section of the *Poetria* seems to reinforce this position:

> Verborum flores et rerum confer in unum
> Area sermonis ut floreat his speciebus
> Florum. Surget enim quidam concursus odorum
> Et redolet plene permixtus uterque colorum.
>   (1584-7)

[Unite the flowers of diction and of things into one so that the field of your discourse may bloom with these species of flowers. For a certain harmony of fragrances will arise and diffuse, both of the colors having been abundantly mixed.]

If his own metaphor will bear the weight of its obvious inter-pretation, Geoffrey ultimately views all the rhetorical devices as means of creating aesthetic enjoyment. They are the "flowers" whose "fragrances" please the senses; they grow from the "field" of subject matter but are not, significantly, part of the very texture of the field itself; nor do they in any way form or mold the soil from which they grow. Yet, we may assume, they will neither flourish nor bloom on unfertile ground. Or, to elaborate his earlier metaphor, the rhetorical devices provide rich robes for the noble matron and make their contribution to her dignified appearance, but they are not an inseparable portion of her essential nature.

In short, despite his condemnation of purely external ornamen-tation, Geoffrey nonetheless does regard the use of rhetorical colors as adornment. He does not recognize, as modern critics would have us do, that style and content are not separable, that the form of expression actually molds what is being expressed, that – in his own metaphor – the "flower" of expression blooms from the PLANT of subject matter, rather than the "field", and is an integral part of that plant, is indeed a major feature which distinguishes it from others of the same genus. Instead, he sees rhetorical devices as a kind of verbal cosmetic, superimposed to create aesthetically pleasing results. However, the poet does not adorn for the sake of adornment, nor amplify for the sake of amplification; rather, he utilizes the colors of rhetoric either, as in Geoffrey's third section, to beautify his utterance or, as in section two, to provide rhetorical emphasis, in order that he may give proper expression to subject matter which is in itself ele-vated, noble, worthy, and valuable. As evidenced by the repeated insistence upon a fitting relationship between thought and form, this goal is not specious or superficial adornment as far as Geof-frey is concerned, but is rather a kind of aesthetic decorum. Lofty subjects deserve a lofty style, just as he has earlier stated that the value of a thought must be equalized by the weight of its ex-pression. Thus, modern scholars who have insisted that the *Poetria Nova* assumes decoration to be the only concern of poetry have not been entirely fair to Geoffrey. Content is equally important, for it is only by a careful balancing of style with content that the decorum which he advocates can be achieved.

Curiously enough, although Geoffrey emphasizes this decorum in general terms, he discusses only one half of the components from which it can be attained. In terms of his image of the weighing balance, he expounds fully the elements which may be placed in one pan but seems to feel no necessity for discussing what goes in the other. The questions, earlier suggested, regarding what he means by "sententia" and "rem" still remain unanswered. It appears that he considers certain kinds of subjects to be inherently worthy of poetic treatment, but because he fails to indicate throughout the major portion of his treatise any *a priori* standards by which subject matter is to be so evaluated, his whole presentation of the idea lacks precision. Only near the end of the third section does he in any way clarify his position. Here, he explicitly states that rhetorical devices are not suitable for the comic:

> Attamen est quandoque color vitare colores,
> Exceptis quos sermo capit vulgaris et usus
> Offert communis. Res comica namque recusat
> Arte laboratos sermones: sola requirit
> Plana.   (1883-7)

[But yet it is sometimes a color to avoid colors, except those which common speech possesses and common usage presents. For certainly a comic thing rejects utterance labored with art: it requires only plain style.]

Yet, even this belated assertion does not adequately explain the matter, for a lavish passage, even though highly serious, may seem to be a purple patch. If we look, however, at the examples which Geoffrey has composed to illustrate all of the various figures and the methods of amplification, we find that the TOPICS chosen fall into certain limited areas of human activity and experience. Description of a regal banquet, of armor, a lament for the death of Richard I; a lament of the Cross, the story of the Fall and Redemption of man, a discussion of the duties of the Pope; metaphorical descriptions of the seasons, of clouds, of winds, of seas; a description of a beautiful woman, of youth, of old age; apostrophes against excessive joy, presumption, ridicule – all these and many others concern the affairs of kings, the practices and doctrines of Christianity, the beauties of nature and of the human being, and the moral and ethical qualities of man, and are, we may assume, noble subjects deserving of poetic (i.e., rhetorical) treatment. Thus, it seems that when Geoffrey speaks of THOUGHT [sententia], he frequently means not only IDEA but also SUBJECT MATTER – at times, indeed, topic RATHER than idea, since many of his examples are pure descriptions which scarcely embody any idea *per se* and which certainly do not convey a didactic concept. "Sententia", therefore, is perhaps best understood in its least precise meaning as simply the thing [rem] about which the poet writes, this thing – be it idea or topic – to be expressed in a level of style properly equated to the level of the material in a hierarchy of poetic subject matter. In Geoffrey's own terms, then, an elaborate description of a beautiful woman is an inherently worthy topic demanding equally worthy expression. A noble matron must not blush in pauper's rags!

If we examine the major prose treatise also attributed to Geoffrey, the *Documentum de modo et arte dictandi et versificandi*,[20] in order to verify these conclusions about his concept of the nature of poetry, we find some additional support, even though the *Documentum* really has little to say about theoretical concerns. This work repeats much of the material found in the *Poetria* and often illustrates points with the same verses; its approach, however, is simplified and far more mechanical, and great attention is given to grammatical problems connected with the various figures. Contrary to his practice in the *Poetria*, Geoffrey here (if

---

[20] Faral, pp. 22-3, discusses the question of Geoffrey's being the author of the *Documentum* and concludes: "En fin d'examen, on ne voit pas qu'il y ait de raisons sérieuses pour contester l'attribution indiquée par le manuscrit de Glasgow et par ceux qui figurent au catalogue de Bernard." Yet, some of the discrepancies DO seem serious: its vast simplification of explanations, its attention to grammatical problems, its use of classical terminology, its overt emphasis on ornamentation, its elementary exercises for composing figures, etc. One wonders whethers the *Documentum* may not be a prose redaction of the *Poetria* based upon Geoffrey's text but written by someone else who desired to make it suitable for a school text.

he is, in fact, the author of the *Documentum*) constantly uses classical rhetorical terms as well as phrases of his own which suggest the ornamental ["ad decorem materiae", "verborum ducit opulentiam", "ornata facilitas", "ornata difficultas"]. Only once does he repeat the insistent injunction of the *Poetria* that the expression must be appropriate to the thought, but when doing so here, he clearly states the idea in terms of adornment:

Sed hoc adjiciendum quod nec facilitas ornata nec difficultas ornata est alicujus ponderis, si ornatus ille sit tantum exterior. Superficies enim verborum ornata, nisi sana et commendabili nobilitetur senten-tia, similis est picturae vili quae placet longius stanti, sed displicet propius intuenti. Sic et ornatus verborum sine ornatu sententiarum audienti placet, diligenti intuenti displicet. Superficies autem ver-borum ornata cum ornatu sententiae similis est egregiae picturae, quae quidem, quando propius inspicitur, tanto commendabilior in-venitur.   (II. iii. 2)

[But it must be added that neither an easy ornament nor a difficult ornament is of any weight if the ornament be merely external. For surface decoration of words, unless ennobled by sound commendable thought, is like a worthless painting which pleases one standing at a distance but displeases one examining it closely. Thus, ornateness of words without ornateness of thought pleases the casual listener but displeases the attentive examiner. However, surface decoration of words with ornateness of thought is like an excellent painting which, when examined closely, is found to be even more commendable.]

Since the poet, like the painter, hopes to produce true art, Geof-frey goes on to offer this advice:

Cogitandum igitur prius est de sententia quam cogitemus de verborum junctura. Mortua sunt enim verba si non incolumi nitantur sententia, quae quodam modo anima est verbi. Cum constiterit de sententia, procedendum est ad verba, diligentiam adhibendo, ut series verborum sit ornata.   (II. iii. 2)

[Therefore, one must first consider the thought before he considers joining words to it. For words are dead if they are not brilliant with sound thought, which is in a certain manner the breath of life of a word. When one has established the thought, he must proceed to the words and apply great care so that the sequence of words be orna-mental.]

This assertion reinforces what the relevant metaphors in the

Poetria imply: namely, that Geoffrey regards thought and expression as separate elements. Even though he here states that thought is the breath of life for a word, he still instructs the poet to consider first the thought and then the words which are to be joined to it.

The passage does not, however, clarify what he means by "thought". When he modifies "sententia" with such adjectives as "sober", "commendable", and "sound", it would seem that he is thinking of ideas rather than topics, yet the methods of procedure which he recommends in various parts of the treatise simply defy any kind of correlation with the concept that "sound, praiseworthy" ideas are the point of origin for poetry. When discussing metaphor, for example, he suggests that the poet make a long list of verbs and adjectives ["scribat infinita verba ... et adjectiva", (II. iii. 8)] and work out all the possible substitutions which can be made among them to create figurative expressions. In this way the poet will become "copiosus in inventione translationum" and can avoid boring his audience with the same old metaphors – "Idemptitas enim mater est satietatis" [Repetition is the mother of satiation]. Even more revealing of paucity of idea is the long section which concludes the discussion of methods of amplification (II. ii. 46-69). Here, Geoffrey takes two words, "lego" and "doceo", which can hardly be considered ideas at all, and shows at great length how various things can be added so that the final results actually do state ideas. The significant point is, of course, that by this process the idea comes last rather than first. Both of these mechanical methods, however, might be applicable if the term "sententia" were construed as "subject-matter", as the *Poetria* suggests that it sometimes should be.

Since this is the only reference to "sententia" in the *Documentum*, Geoffrey's intention remains debatable; however, a passage near the end of the work offers material which is not found in the *Poetria* and which seems relevant to the question. Among various precepts for which the authority of Horace is cited, Geoffrey introduces the idea of the three styles – high, middle, and low – and repeats the old adage that Virgil's *Aeneid*, *Georgics*, and *Eclogues* illustrate the three respectively. The styles

have received these names, he writes, because of the subject
matter each treats:

Sunt igitur tres styli, humilis, mediocris, grandiloquus. Et tales reci-
piunt appellationes styli ratione personarum vel rerum de quibus fit
tractatus. Quando enim de generalibus personis vel rebus tractatur,
tunc est stylus grandiloquus: quando de humilibus, humilis; quando
de mediocribus, mediocris.   (II. iii. 145)

He goes on to discuss the faults commonly linked with each
style: the high may be turgid and inflated because of metaphors
which are too uncultivated and bombastic ["nimis duris et am-
pullosis utitur translationibus"]; the middle may be wavering and
shifting ["dissolutum et fluitans"] because it slides in and out of
both the high and low styles; the low may be dry and lifeless
["aridus et exsanguis"] because it uses a contemptible lightness
or shallowness ["nimis contemptibili et vili utitur levitate"]. The
faults are interchangeable among the three styles, however, because not all poets observe the major dictum that a uniform style
should be maintained:

Tertio, considerandum est ut stylum materiae non variemus, id est ut
de grandiloquo stylo non descendamus ad humilem . . . . Sed et de
humili stylo non ascendamus ad grandiloquum stylum; similiter nec
de mediocri declinandum est ad alterutrum illorum, immo quocumque
stylo velimus utatur, dummodo in materia servemus uniformitatem
styli et sic declinemus a vitio styli, quod dicit Horatius hoc versu:
"Denique sit quod vis, simplex dumtaxat et unum."
                                          (II. iii. 157)

The fact that the basis for choice of one of the three styles is
subject matter [21] supports the conjecture that when Geoffrey

[21] Such was not the case in classical rhetoric. St. Augustine, for example,
discusses the three styles in terms of the speaker's purpose: the low style
is best for instruction, the middle for pleasing, the high for moving the
audience to action (De Doctrina, IV.17.34). Faral, pp. 86-7, states that in
antiquity the division of expression into three styles "repose sur les qualités
de l'élocution et d'elle seule. C'est bien ainsi que l'entend encore Isidore
(De rhetorica, 17). Mais, de bonne heure déjà, elle a été interprétée de
façon différente. Dans les Scholia vindobonensia ad Horatii Artem poeti-
cam, qui émanent peut-être d'un critique de l'école d'Alcuin et qui sont,
en tout cas, antérieures au XIe siècle, on lit . . . 'Humile genus est, si
quando res viles sibi convenientibus vocibus designantur, ut cum qui diceret
ardentem testam: ecce vilem rem, id est testam, proprio nomine nominavit.

speaks of correlating expression with thought, he actually refers to what our age calls the topic. The *Documentum* is not very precise in indicating the difference between the three levels of subject matter, but we do learn that topics dealing with man and the world in the abstract or universal sense ["generalibus personis vel rebus"] demand the high style and that ordinary people and things should be discussed in the middle style, low persons or topics in the low. The comic, here as in the *Poetria*, is considered low. This perversion of the classical idea of three styles was common during the Middle Ages. John of Garland (c. 1180-1252), for example, gives a somewhat different division of subject matter when discussing the concept in his *Poetria*, but the topic is still the factor which determines the level of style:

Item sunt tres stili secundum tres status hominum; pastorali vite convenit stilus humilis, agricolis mediocris, gravis gravibus personis que presunt pastoribus et agricolis. . . .[22]

[Also there are three styles following the three states of mankind; the low style is fitting for the life of shepherds, the middle for that of farmers, the high for that of important people who rank above shepherds and farmers.]

The elaborate expression achieved through abundant use of rhetorical devices is obviously the high style; yet, from the *Documentum* we learn that metaphor may appear in any style ["cum in quolibet stylo utimur translationibus" (II. iii. 150)], and, as Geoffrey here states, two rhetorical colors are appropriate for the comic: *occupatio* ['quando dicimus nos nolle dicere quod dicimus" (II. iii. 167)] and *praecisio* or unfinished sentence. This assertion is more precise than what the *Poetria* says on the subject; however, the discussion of levels of style generally supports the conclusions about decorum drawn from that work.

Mediocre est, ut si dicas *lucernam*, quia lucerna non tantum minorum sicut testa est, sed etiam majorum. Grave est si dixeris *aureos lychnos*, quia pertinent tantum ad potentes.' On remarque qu'ici la distinction entre styles implique une distinction entre les qualités des personnes dont il s'agit. C'est un acheminement vers la doctrine enseignée par nos arts et que Geoffroi exprime" in the *Documentum*.
[22] John of Garland, *Poetria*, ed. Giovanni Mari, *Romanische Forschungen*, XIII (1902), 920.

Geoffrey is the only one of the medieval theorists who really justifies the use of rhetorical colors as an essential ingredient of aesthetic decorum operating within a hierarchical concept of "worthiness" of poetic subject matter.[23] Matthew of Vendôme, for example, makes no attempt to correlate thought and expression but instead bluntly asserts that style and content are separate things in poetry. In the dream which introduces part II of his *Ars Versificatoria*, Matthew learns from Elegy, one of the hand-maidens of Philosophy, that the poet's art consists of three things – beauty of thought, surface embellishment of words, method of expression – and that the charm of a poem comes not from a union of the three but from ONE OR THE OTHER of them:

> Elegia audita est mihi propalare tripartitam versificatoriae facultatis elegantiam. Etenim sunt tria quae redolent in carmine: verba polita, dicendique color, interiorque favus. Versus enim aut contrahit elegan-tiam ex venustate interioris sententiae, aut ex superficiali ornatu ver-borum, aut ex modo dicendi.   (II. 8-9)

Of the three elements, Matthew is concerned almost exclusively with the latter two. To develop the concept of beauty of thought, which for him clearly denotes idea, he devotes one short para-graph to commentary upon single epigrammatical lines from Horace and Lucan. These are examples of verse in which the charm must be considered to arise from the thought, he says, since the language is colloquial [verba quotidiana] and no tropes or rhetorical figures [scemata] appear! After this terse and bril-

---

[23] John of Garland considers subject matter in the first major section of his *Poetria*, ed. Mari (note 22), pp. 887-93, but his treatise so intermingles letter writing (*ars dictaminis*) with poetry that it is impossible to deter-mine to what extent he intends this section to apply to poetry. He says that subject matter must be subjected to five questions: *ubi, quid, quale, qualiter*, and *ad quid*. WHERE (*ubi*) subject matter exists is in persons, exempla, and etymology; WHAT (*quid*) it consists of in relation to these three areas is largely a question of moral or ethical values (e.g. does a king rule well or ruin his country by tyranny); OF WHAT SORT in relation to subject matter is specifically whether it is good or bad; TO WHAT END is virtue and utility. In so far as this discussion may relate to poetry, the HOW (which includes amplification and rhetorical colors) serves to express didactic concepts, which would certainly fit into Geoffrey's less specific idea of "worthiness" of poetic subject matter.

liantly inadequate discussion of thought,[24] Matthew then analyzes the problem of words and expression throughout the remainder of part II and all of part III, thus revealing his preponderant concern with surface embellishment.

Although Geoffrey's demand for equating level of style with level of subject is valid enough within its own limitations, the foundations upon which it rests have been vehemently denied in our own century. There is no such thing as an inherently poetic subject matter, we insist, and to regard form and content as separate or separable elements in poetry is fallacious. If our contemporary judgments are correct, Geoffrey's poetic theory is basically wrong in these respects, but at least he and his medieval cohorts have a host of later theorists to help them bear the burden of their error.

Right or wrong, it is within the framework of such a concept of the nature of poetry that Geoffrey discusses imagery. As stated before, several of the traditional rhetorical figures produce what we would now call imagery, although they are not separated from completely non-imagistic figures in any of the various classification systems devised for discussing this aspect of style. The two-fold division of figures used in the *Rhetorica ad Herennium*, for example, lists a device with the *exornationes verborum* if it results primarily from word play and with the *exornationes sententiarum* if it results from choice of material. Thus, metaphor appears in the former classification because the words are not to be taken literally, simile in the latter because the comparison is contained in an added phrase. Geoffrey, however, includes three devices connected with imagery – comparison, personification, and description – along with such things as repetition, circumlocution, and apostrophe in his discussion of methods of amplification in the second section of the *Poetria*.

If the previous conclusions about his theory of amplification

---

[24] Faral indicates in his marginalia that he considers part I, which discusses ways of beginning a poem and techniques of description, to be devoted to "thought" in poetry, and this may be what Matthew intended, although the distinction is by no means so clear-cut as Faral suggests. It is true, however, that portions of Matthew's material in part I are drawn from the *inventio* aspect of classical rhetoric.

are correct, then these three devices all serve as means of providing proper emphasis for worthy material, although Geoffrey
does not explicitly incorporate his original concept of purpose into
the ensuing passages. The discussion of comparison (241-63) does
little more than to suggest it as a third means of amplification
and to distinguish between simile and metaphor: "collatio, facta
biformi/ Lege: vel occulte, vel aperte" (241-2) [comparison,
made by a twofold method: either covertly or openly]. The
"collatio aperta" indicates likeness, he says, by three explicit
signs: "more than", "less than", and "like":

> collatio quae fit aperte
> Se gerit in specie simili, quam signa revelant
> Expresse. Tria sunt haec signa: magis, minus, aeque.
>
> (244-6)

Thus, he includes in this device not only the simile but also the
comparative degree of the adjective, which may or may not
produce an image. The metaphor he explains as a comparison
not openly indicated by such signs, but rather one in which the
thing borrowed has been so implanted by a marvellous trans-
formation as to seem to be inherent in the subject, not imported
from without:

> Sumpta tamen res est aliunde, sed esse videtur
> Inde; foris res est, nec ibi comparet; et intus
> Apparet, sed ibi non est; sic fluctuat intus
> Et foris, hic et ibi, procul et prope; distat et astat.
>
> (252-5)

This definition is somewhat lacking in clarity, but since he returns to metaphor at length in the third section of his work, he
allows it to stand here with a few laudatory examples, and he
offers no instruction concerning its use other than to indicate
that the two elements intermingled in the metaphor must seem
to be joined by the hand of nature rather than the hand of art
["sic continue quasi non manus artis/ Junxerit, immo manus
naturae" (261-2)]. The phrasing used in this line foreshadows his
later warnings against forced comparisons, but he in no way
suggests that either metaphor or simile can function in any other
way within a poem than as a means of amplifying or dignifying

the subject matter. He concludes the passage by stating that the metaphor is preferable to the "open" comparison because it requires more art and has a more distinguished usage ["Plus habet artis/ Hic modus, est in eo longe sollemnior usus" (261-2)].

Personification, the fifth technique for amplification ["ultra protendere cursum' (461)], also differs somewhat from its modern definition. Geoffrey invokes the instructress Prosopopeia, whom he describes as "Cui nulla potentia fandi,/ Da licite fari donetque licentia linguam" (462-3). As both this statement and the three succeeding "new" examples which are given indicate, personification for Geoffrey is limited to speeches made by inanimate objects.[25] The only function either mentioned or implied is that of stretching out the course of the poem, in order, we may presume, that the value of the thought may be equalized by the weight of the expression.

In the discussion of description, the seventh of eight devices suggested for amplification, Geoffrey so frequently reiterates the idea of expansiveness that it almost seems as if he thinks that copious description in itself possesses beauty and is capable of delighting the mind:

> Septima succedit *praegnans* descriptio verbis,
> Ut *dilatet* opus. Sed, cum sit *lata*, sit ipsa
> Laeta: pari forma speciosa sit et *spatiosa.*
> In *celebri* forma faciat res nubere verbis
> Si cibus esse velit et *plena* refectio mentis,
> *Ne sit curta nimis brevitas vel trita vetustas.*
> Sint variata novis exempla secuta figuris,
> Rebus ut in variis oculus *spatietur* et auris.
>
> (554-61)

[The seventh instructress, description pregnant with words, follows so that the work may expand. But, although she be extended, let her

---

[25] This is not precisely true of the figure (*conformatio*) as it is defined in the *ad Herennium*: "Conformatio est cum aliqua quae non adest persona confingitur quasi adsit, aut cum res muta aut informis fit eloquens, et *forma* ei et oratio adtribuitur ad dignitatem adcommodata aut *actio* quaedam." (IV, liii, 66). Although speech is emphasized here and the two succeeding examples are dialogue, the author does include within the figure the attributing of human form and action (without speech) to things not human.

be pleasing: let her be equally beautiful and broad in figure. Let the thing be covered in a renowned beauty of words. If it wishes to be nourishment and a full restoration for the mind, let its brevity not be too short nor its duration of time trite. Let the following examples serve as varieties of a new kind so that your eye and ear may promenade over various things.]

The beauty recommended, however, is not synonymous with dilation; the poet must see that the two are combined. Since beauty of expression is the subject of the third section of his treatise, Geoffrey does not here elaborate the idea further, but goes on to an illustrative example which describes the face and body of a woman, the details following a prescribed order descending from head to feet ["A summo capitis descendat splendor ad ipsam/ Radicem" (598-9)]. Such descriptions of people and of their clothes (his second example) are very common in poetry, he notes, and the key to the successful use of the device is the poet's care in insuring that all is embellished perfectly ["totumque simul poliatur ad unguem" (599)]. He concludes his rather lengthy discussion of this method (117 lines) with a description of a regal banquet, which he states is a type of subject less frequently so adorned with words than is the human figure. As previously suggested, these examples are impossible to correlate with his initial statement regarding the purpose of amplification unless "sententia" can be considered to mean "topic", and his enthusiasm for language conveying notions of expansiveness makes it easy to forget that this technique supposedly serves a deeper purpose.

Description is more fully discussed by Matthew of Vendôme, who devotes two-thirds of part I of the *Ars Versificatoria* to it, and who sets forth a concept of purpose unique among medieval theorists.[26] For Geoffrey, description serves appropriately to beautify worthy material and give it proper emphasis; for Matthew, however, descriptive passages must function in some meaningful way in terms of the particular context:

Et notandum quod . . . descriptio loci vel temporis plerumque potest esse superflua, plerumque opportuna. Nisi enim temporis aut loci

[26] Faral, p. 77.

amminiculo aliquid auditori velimus intimare, supersedendum erit
loci descriptioni . . . .   (I. 110)
[And it must be recognized that description of place or of season can
frequently be superfluous, frequently serviceable. Truly, unless we
wish to intimate something to the listener by the corroborative evidence of season or place, description of place must be omitted.]

He offers three illustrations of this "intimating something to the
listener". Referring to Lucan's description of Cato (*Pharsalia*,
II, 380 ff.), he asserts that the original portrait which establishes
Cato's austerity, manliness, and refinement of manners is necessary so that what follows in regard to Caesar's disrespect ["quic-
quid sequatur de negligentia Caesaris" (I. 39)] may be more
easily presented in an acceptable way. The auditor, in other
words, gains a favorable impression of Cato which subsequently
facilitates the depiction of Caesar in a negative light. So also, if
the poet wishes to show Jupiter burning with love for Paras, an
initial description of the beauty of the girl will make the infatuation seem real ["verisimile sit" (I. 40)]; and, similarly, the passage
in the *Verrine Orations* in which Cicero describes the place in
Sicily where Verres committed adultery, serves to make the
commission of the sin seem likely because it presents the manifold
charms of the setting in which the act was alleged to have occurred (I. 110). These examples show that by "purpose" Matthew
means some specific integral function rather than mere appropriateness. Unfortunately, however, the original descriptive passages which he composes for the *Ars Versificatoria* are isolated
units which cannot illustrate his concept of purpose since they
have no surrounding context. As a result, scholars have tended to
depreciate his assertions. Even Faral, who calls this a "précepte
judicieux", says: "En fait, dans les exemples qu'en offre la
littérature, elle (i.e. description) est souvent oiseuse; chez beau-
coup d'auteurs, et chez Matthieu lui-même, elle fait plus d'une
fois hors-d'oeuvre et n'a d'autre raison d'être que l'observance
d'une tradition routinière." [27] Nevertheless, the fact that Matthew
even preaches such a doctrine is significant, for it indicates a
truer awareness of the relationship of technique to effect than

[27] *Ibid.*

anything found in Geoffrey's works. Yet, oddly enough, Matthew does not apply the same idea to any of the other rhetorical devices, and his discussions of words, tropes, and rhetorical colors in no way indicates how they serve any purpose other than adornment. This inconsistency may perhaps be explained by the fact that he draws many of his ideas about description from Cicero's *De Inventione,* where the materials are presented as possible sources for formulating convincing arguments in legal trials. In this context, the necessity for relevance of anything used to the purpose of the whole pleading is obvious, and Matthew seems simply to have adapted the idea from classical judicial rhetoric to his aesthetic theory. The traditional figures of style, however, are discussed from a different point of view in classical rhetoric. In the *ad Herennium,* for example, they are simply embellishments which give "dignitas" to composition, "dignitas" being distinction resulting from varied ornamentation ["Dignitas est quae reddit ornatum orationem varietate distinguens" (IV, xiii, 18)], and Matthew treats them in the same way. Indeed, the statement which Elegy makes in part II suggests that Matthew considers ornamentation itself a major purpose since it is one of the three sources of poetic charm ["ex superficiali ornatu verborum"]. Whatever the case, Matthew was not sufficiently perceptive to see that the concept of integral function could apply to other poetic devices than description, even though he incorporates into his initial definition of poetry the statement that a poem contains nothing alienated, nothing idle ["quae nihil diminutum, nihil in se continet otiosum" (I. 1)].

Matthew's illustrative descriptions of people follow the same stylized order of presentation advocated by Geoffrey, from the head downward ["a summo capitis . . . ad ipsam radicem"], but he makes a clear distinction between the visual portrait (*effictio*) and the figure which the *ad Herennium* calls *notatio* – description of character:

Et notandum quod cujuslibet personae duplex potest esse descriptio: una superficialis, alia intrinseca; superficialis, quando membrorum elegantia describitur vel homo exterior, intrinseca, quando interioris hominis proprietates, scilicet ratio, fides, patientia, honestas, injuria, superbia, luxuria et cetera epitheta interioris hominis, scilicet animae, ad laudem vel ad vituperium exprimuntur.   (I. 74)

[And it must be recognized that there can be two kinds of description of any person whatever: one surface, the other inward; surface when the grace of the limbs or the exterior man is described, inward when the properties of the inner man are described, namely reasonableness, faith, patience, honesty, injustice, pride, excess, and other epithets of the inner man, that is to say of the soul, in order to express either praise or blame.]

None of the examples which he gives intermingles the two types. The descriptions of Ulysses, Caesar, a pope, Davus, and Marcia contain no visual details, while the portraits of Helen and the hag Beroe are primarily visual.[28] Like the illustrative *effictio* in the *Poetria Nova*, the description of Helen presents an idealized image of feminine beauty which is in no way individualized. Similarly, the disgusting details which are applied to Beroe combine into an epitome of ugliness which is equally unrealistic. This concern for the generic is evident in all of Matthew's descriptions. His seasons are typical; his garden contains such a variety of birds as to defy all verisimilitude. The object in description, then, is to pile up details ("Description rejoices in a parade [pompa] of words", says Eberhard, l. 329) which will convey the essence of a pre-determined generalization. For people, this intention subdivides into the two broad categories of praise or censure, which stem from the principal objects of the classical genre of demonstrative or epideictic oratory as described by Quintilian and others, and which recur in discussions of judicial oratory as modes of winning favor for or disparaging witnesses. Censure, Matthew asserts, should be used less frequently than praise because the unanimity of human frailties bends low toward the censurable, and emphasizing the positive will provide better doctrinal instruction:

Etenim in exprimendo vituperio parcior debet esse instructio doctrinalis, ad quod vergit declivior consensus humanae fragilitatis.
                    (I. 59)

---

[28]   The fact that his two *effictios* describe women and the men are treated in *notatios* is in accord with his assertion that it is fitting to expand upon the physical beauty of a woman but not upon that of a man (I.67).

His assertion here suggests rather strongly that Matthew regards all poetry as serving a moral purpose, as inculcating Christian teaching, but it is difficult to find any hint of this idea outside his statements about descriptions of people.

Because the aim in description is the epitome rather than the particular, Matthew frequently discusses stereotyped epithets which should be used for various topics. He also devotes much space to a system of attributes, taken from Cicero's *De Inventione:*

Sunt igitur attributa personae undecim: nomen, natura, convictus, fortuna, habitus, studium, affectio, consilium, casus, facta, orationes.

(I. 77)

[There are therefore eleven attributes of person: name, nature, mode of life, fortune, habits, interests, feelings, intentions, accidents, deeds, and speech.]

These are the things which a poet should include when describing a person, but they apply primarily to the *notatio.* Only "affectio" when reflected by the body and "natura" include visual imagery ["Hoc autem attributum (i.e. nature) juxta Tullium tripartito dividitur, scilicet in attributa quae sumuntur *a corpore* et in illa quae sumuntur ab anima" (I. 79)], and Matthew merely gives examples of these.[29] Thus, his doctrine on the use of descriptions combines a unique concept of their function with formalized, conventional patterns for their composition. Nothing which he says in this section suggests that he regards description, as do Geoffrey and the other rhetoricians, as a means of amplification.

In the third section of the *Poetria Nova,* that devoted to making the words of a poem "civil rather than barbarous", Geoffrey

[29] Matthew also applies two of Cicero's four classes for attributes of things to description, but the discussion contributes nothing to our understanding of description as imagery. Of this section, Derek A. Pearsall, "Rhetorical 'Descriptio' in Sir Gawain and the Green Knight", *Modern Language Review,* L (1955), 129-30, writes: "These [attributes], it would seem, have specifically to do with *inventio,* and cannot be transferred to description. Nevertheless, Matthew attempts to do so, and Cicero is sadly mauled in the process. Illogical as it is, Matthew's treatment remains important, in particular because it gives rhetorical justification for the *descriptio temporis* and the *descriptio loci* from the attributes of time and place." It lends the "weight of classical doctrine" to such descriptions.

provides some additional information about figures relevant to imagery. Returning to metaphor, he now presents it as a means of providing appropriate adornment for "rich thought" rather than as a technique for properly amplifying the subject. He no longer speaks of the device as a hidden comparison ["collatio occulta"] but rather as the seemly adaption of words ["modus transsumere verba decenter" (765)], sometimes discussing this "transsumptio" from the point of view of subject matter, sometimes in terms of parts of speech. His whole concept is essentially elementary, despite the fine points of distinction which he attempts to establish upon such bases as whether metaphor results from "transsuming" a noun, a verb, or an adjective, or whether the word "transsumed" precedes or follows the "fixed" term.[30] His only major point is that one can create a metaphor by adapting to human beings words customarily applied to inanimate objects ("dentes *nivei*"; "frons *lactea*", 773-4), or vice versa ('Tempora veris/ *Pingere* flore solum" (791-2), or by adapting a word from one object to another ('Sermonem discute quis sit/ *Crudus* an *excoctus*", 910-11), or from one aspect of human activity to another ("Quid aget rex noster *inermis*/ Consiliis, *cinctus* odiis, et *nudus* amicis?", 914-5). His exposition of this concept, however, lacks the terse simplicity of the statement of the same idea which appears in Matthew's *Ars Versificatoria*:

Metaphora est alicujus verbi usurpata translatio. Hic autem tropus quadripertito dividitur. Fit enim plerumque ab animato ad animatum, ab inanimato ad inanimatum, ab animato ad inanimatum, ab inanimato ad animatum.   (III. 19)

In making this four-part division, of course, both rhetoricians incorporate what is now defined as personification into metaphor "ab animato ad inanimatum".[31] Because of the length of Geoffrey's discussion of this device (180 lines) as well as his earlier

---

[30] Geoffrey's discussion here reflects the fusion of stylistic figures with the study of grammar.

[31] The *ad Herennium* says nothing of these four elementary ways of creating metaphor. It defines the figure thus: Translatio est cum verbum in quandam rem transferetur ex alia re, quod propter similitudinem recte videbitur posse transferri. (IV, xxxiv, 45.) It also offers several motives for using the figure, including the desire to create a mental image ("rei ante oculos ponendae causa").

explanation and his statement that it is preferable to the "open" comparison, metaphor appears to be one of his favorite modes of poetic expression; and Matthew openly recommends it above all other tropes as a source of poetic beauty:

Iste siquidem tropus quadam speciali praerogativa inter ceteros tropos singularem obtinet praeminentiam et maxime a versificatoribus debet frequentari: praecipuam enim metricae modulationi venustatem accommodat. (III. 24)

Interestingly enough, modern critics have given metaphor this same preeminence albeit upon rather different grounds.

The other figures which Geoffrey includes in his third section are treated briefly, most of his presentation of the *exornationes sententiarum* being devoted to a long passage on the duties of the Pope, in which he uses the various devices in the order in which they are discussed in the *ad Herennium*. Before he offers this illustration, however, he mentions the figures about to be employed and gives terse explanations. For the *similitudo* of the *ad Herennium*, he writes, "Saepius ex re/ Dissimili similem traho" (1254-5); *imago*, on the other hand, is comparison of like things (1258-9); *effictio* is description of physical appearance (1260-1); *demonstratio* is presentation of an event so that the reader receives a clear mental image ["Ut quasi sit praesens oculis" (1273)].[32] Geoffrey obviously wants merely to call his reader's attention to familiar material; indeed, he says in line 1251 that all this is treated fully in Cicero. From both his definitions and his succeeding illustration, we learn only that such types of imagery are regarded as clearly defined figures, to be employed consciously by the poet. Geoffrey says nothing about the function of these devices except that they allow the thought to shine obliquely ["Lucet ab obliquo" (1582)].

The sum total of these scattered passages indicates that for Geoffrey imagery serves only one basic function. The relevant

[32] *Descriptio*, in both the *ad Herennium* and Geoffrey's definition is lucid explanation of the consequences of an action. When this term is used for a figure of thought, it is not connected with imagery, as its name would seem to suggest. The common noun "descriptio", however, is often used in a general rather than a specific sense to mean "description", as is the case in the *Poetria Nova*, II, 554.

figures are used, as are all the techniques of rhetoric, to beautify and/or emphasize material worthy of such treatment; and, in terms of Geoffrey's perception, the only necessity, indeed possibility, is that the image have a surface appropriateness which observes the proper decorum. Never does he show the least awareness that an image can extend its meaning beyond its immediate point of reference or that the nature of all the imagery can modify the total meaning of a passage or of a poem as a whole. Yet, unlike many of his contemporary theorists, Geoffrey reveals some sense of the wholeness of a work of art. He begins his treatise with an analogy which correlates the poet with the builder of a house; before starting to build, each must lay out a plan whose parts are carefully measured and ordered:

> Si quis habet fundare domum, non currit ad actum
> Impetuosa manus: intrinseca linea cordis
> Praemetitur opus, seriemque sub ordine certo
> Interior praescribit homo, totamque figurat
> Ante manus cordis quam corporis; et status ejus
> Est prius archetypus quam sensilis. Ipsa poesis
> Spectet in hoc speculo quae lex sit danda poetis.
> Non manus ad calamum praeceps, non lingua sit ardens
> Ad verbum: neutram manibus committe regendam
> Fortunae; sed mens discreta praeambula facti,
> Ut melius fortunet opus, suspendat earum
> Officium, tractetque diu de themate secum.
> Circinus interior mentis praecircinet omne
> Materiae spatium . . . .
>   Opus totum prudens in pectoris arcem
> Contrahe, sitque prius in pectore quam sit in ore.
> Mentis in arcano cum rem digesserit ordo,
> Materiam verbis veniat vestire poesis.
> Quando tamen servire venit, se praeparet aptam
> Obsequio dominae: caveat sibi, ne caput hirtis
> Crinibus, aut corpus pannosa veste, vel ulla
> Ultima displiceant, alicunde nec inquinet illud
> Hanc poliens partem: pars si qua sedebit inepte,
> Tota trahet series ex illa parte pudorem:
> Fel modicum totum mel amaricat; unica menda
> Totalem faciem difformat. Cautius ergo
> Consule materiae, ne possit probra vereri.

(43-70)

[If someone has to build a house, he should not rush into action with impetuous hands: the work should be measured beforehand by the internal plumb-line of the heart; the inner man should prescribe its sequence in a fixed order and shape the whole with the hands of his heart before he does so with the hands of his body; its state is first imagined before it is made visible to the senses. Poetry herself may observe in this analogy the law which must be given to poets. Let there be no hand rushing headlong to the pen, no tongue burning for the word; entrust the government of neither of these two to the hands of chance. Rather, so that the work may fare the better, let the discerning mind pace slowly in advance of the action; let it check the services of the pen and the tongue, and treat the theme a long time within itself. Let an internal pair of compasses within the mind completely inscribe the circumference of the material in advance . . . . Judiciously draw together the whole work within the vault of the heart and let it be first in the heart before it be in the mouth. When the order has arranged the thing within the secret chamber of the mind, then let it come forth to dress the matter in the words of poetry. Yet, when she comes to serve, let her with deference prepare herself fittingly for her mistress (i.e. the poetic material): let her beware lest a head of shaggy hair or a body clothed in rags, or any least thing be displeasing; nor let her, while polishing this part, defile that part from anywhere: if there be any part which sits inappropriately, the whole sequence draws shame from that part. A modicum of gall embitters all the honey; one blemish deforms the whole face. Therefore, look to the subject matter the more carefully so that it need not fear insults.]

That this is hardly comparable to Coleridge's organic unity is obvious, yet the concern for an ordered scope in which the parts are suitably adapted to the total "sequence" indicates a certain awareness of the aesthetic whole. Geoffrey envisions the rhetorical devices, which make up the bulk of his treatise, as providing the fitting exterior for the basic plan. Yet, he never asks how a specific figure may operate within the whole. Always, the implication is that a rhetorical device is relevant only to its immediate context, where it serves to express the "sententia" in an aesthetically pleasing manner.

One final point connected with the simile appears in Matthew's *Ars Versificatoria*, and although of no great import, it is rather interesting. In part IV, when he mentions reworking ancient stories, he states that the "modern" poet should follow the course [tenorem] of the original but should not include certain "collateralia" which are not "de principali proposito". The comparison, or simile, is one such "collateralium" which he considers to be an artificial addition greatly favored by the ancients to augment a paucity of truly poetic material:

... ut materiae penuria poetico figmento plenius exuberans in artificosum luxuriaret incrementum. Hoc autem modernis non licet.

(IV. 5)[33]

It is difficult to understand why Matthew could accept lengthy descriptions as being intrinsic to a poem and yet consider similes artificial, but one suspects his judgment in this matter of being biased by the general taste of his age. As Faral points out, the epic simile fell out of favor at the end of the eleventh century,[34] and although Matthew does not specify what kind of comparison he means, he is very probably thinking of what the *ad Herennium* defines as "similtudo per conlationem" (IV, xlvii, 60), in which two grammatically separate elements are juxtaposed in parallel structure, as contrasted with the simile "per brevitatem", in which the comparison occurs within one grammatical construction, the "like" or "as" being used as a preposition.

This aversion to the simile is echoed by other medieval writers on poetics, although no one else attempts to justify his taste on such dubious grounds. As mentioned above, Geoffrey merely defines the simile in the *Poetria Nova* and states a preference for metaphor. In the *Documentum* he devotes one paragraph to explaining simile as a form of digression (and hence as a means of amplification) and he concludes with the statement that since an infinite number of examples can be found in previous poetic works, he will pass it by briefly (II, ii, 21). In the *Laborintus* Eberhard also lists comparison as a device for amplification, but he recommends that it be used infrequently and then only in a simple form:

[33] Because of this passage and other such slighting references to the ancients, Curtius, p. 490, has called Matthew a *modernus* and described him as the first theoretician who consciously wants to be "modern".
[34] Faral, pp. 69-70.

Solemnis fuerat quondam collatio multis;
    Sed nunc, quando venit, rara, modesta venit:
    Non sine spineto crescit rosa; nec sine mundi
    Tormento Domino vita placere potest.

(313-16)

For both Geoffrey and Eberhard, the simile seems to be in disrepute simply because it has been overworked by ancient authors. Yet, Geoffrey, unlike Matthew and Eberhard, does not insist that it should be used sparingly.

Such, then, is the doctrine expounded by the medieval writers on poetics in regard to imagery. The poet is instructed to employ with infinite care the seven figures – *conformatio, effictio, notatio, demonstratio, imago, similitudo,* and *translatio* – to amplify or adorn his subject. Only Matthew and Geoffrey imply any other purpose for rhetorical devices, and in the case of Matthew the exception applies to description alone, the other figures being discussed purely in terms of ornamentation. Geoffrey, by contrast, demands decorum; the figures are not to be used for their own sake but rather for beautifying or emphasizing worthy "thoughts", by which, it seems, he frequently means topics. For all the writers, style and content are separate things in poetry, and the emphasis in all their treatises lies heavily on defining, categorizing, and explaining HOW to compose the various figures. The means suggested are often, as in the case of description of people, highly stylized and formulaic. Only Geoffrey and Matthew show any signs of a concept of the wholeness of a poem, and although Geoffrey discusses the matter briefly, he does not consider how the techniques of imagery may function in terms of such an aesthetic whole. Matthew overtly recognizes the concept only in his definition of poetry, where he states that a poem contains "nothing alienated, nothing idle"; but his demand for descriptions which serve some intrinsic purpose for their specific contexts reveals a unique awareness of the entire poem. With this one exception, everything which is said about imagery implies that, at best, a figure has no more than an immediate, surface appropriateness. The tenor of all the treatises is to codify a body of possible modes for poetic expression, and no one except Geoffrey and Gervais gives any indication of realizing that technique alone will not make a poet.

Yet, we must not forget that these men were not writing poetic theory in the modern sense. They were not explaining poetry as it already exists but were offering practical instruction to those who desired to create poems not yet formulated. To abstract from their instruction a rudimentary theory of poetry, as the previous analysis has done, is in a sense to violate their intention, but such a violation seems useful for the present purposes. We must keep in mind, however, when we compare Chaucer's practices with the concepts found in these medieval poetic treatises, that we are juxtaposing materials taken from before and after the fact. That the production of a true poet, a poet in whom Geoffrey's *ignis ingenii* undeniably burned, would surpass any sort of instructional guide-lines which could be codified is only to be expected. That Chaucer knew these guide-lines, however, is undeniable. Even the most casual reader of the *Canterbury Tales* realizes that the various denials of rhetorical powers which Chaucer puts into the mouths of his characters are ironic, and when one comes to the *Tales* fresh from an examination of the poetic treatises, the vast amount of Chaucer's material which echoes the precepts of the theorists is truly astounding. Yet, Chaucer had the power to transcend the conventional even as he adhered to its essential forms. If we approach his poetry armed with such knowledge of medieval poetic concepts as Geoffrey and others can give us, we are then perhaps prepared to face the real challenge of Chaucer's artistry. We can attempt to discover how the poet in practice has transformed the conventional formulae so that they do not appear to be rhetorical devices at all but intimate portions of the organic whole of a given poem; and this process, like the analyses of the New Critics, can illuminate the work of art itself as well as the artistry of its composition.

PART TWO

IMAGERY: SELECTED CANTERBURY TALES IN RELATION TO CHAUCER'S SOURCES AND ANALOGUES

III

INTRODUCTION TO A CHAUCERIAN TECHNIQUE

The foregoing analysis of the medieval doctrine of imagery has reiterated, perhaps *ad nauseam*, the phrase "the concept of the whole", not merely because modern aesthetics has placed special emphasis upon form and structure but because so many medieval literary works seem to develop with a kind of diffuseness which defies neat structural analysis. One need hardly think twice in order to marshal formidable names to disprove this generalization – Dante's *Divine Comedy*, *Sir Gawain and the Green Knight* – yet the structural artistry of these masterpieces represents an awareness of aesthetic unity the more remarkable for its rarity in medieval literature. Works equally distinguished for a host of quite different reasons can be summoned to testify for the opposite side. To my knowledge, no modern critic has yet possessed the ingenuity to explain adequately the relationship of the various parts of *Piers Plowman*, for example; nor does Jean de Meun's portion of the *Roman de la Rose* prove more tractable. Malory's *Morte Darthur* affords perhaps an even more disheartening example, for the brilliant and persuasive analysis of its structural unity which Vida Scudder set forth in 1917 [1] has since been rendered dubious by the discovery in 1934 of the Winchester MS and the evidence therein provided that Malory himself probably composed his work as eight separate, independent romances.[2]

The *Canterbury Tales* has offered modern scholars and critics

---

[1] Vida Scudder, *Le Morte Darthur of Sir Thomas Malory and Its Sources* (New York, 1917).
[2] See: *The Works of Sir Thomas Malory*, ed. Eugene Vinaver, I (Oxford, 1947), vi-lviii.

a particularly tantalizing problem in this respect. Was Chaucer working toward a unified whole, developing some sort of panoramic theme, in which all of the various tales would play their supporting parts? Or was he, like most medieval writers, adding, expanding, digressing as his fancy led him? Would his finished work have embodied some ultimate statement on life, or would it have remained a brilliant framework providing adequate cause for the linking together of some equally brilliant but separated tales? It is not my purpose to consider this unanswerable question, but rather to demonstrate that in a number of the separate tales themselves Chaucer does reveal a unique awareness of the aesthetic whole and that his handling of imagery within these tales contributes significantly to the essential unity of each. The technique which Chaucer developed for the use of imagery in some of his later works correlates with a careful imposition of artistic order upon his narrative materials, and in this practice he transcends both contemporary theory and typical medieval literary production. In other words, he as poet, and perhaps as unavowed theorist, has taken the step which neither Geoffrey of Vinsauf nor Matthew of Vendôme completed: he has asked and answered the question of how the rhetorically oriented techniques of imagery may function within the aesthetic whole of an individual poem, and the answer which he has evolved, as succeeding chapters will attempt to show, both depends upon and reinforces a concept of organic wholeness. That such is the case for some of the individual tales may, indeed, encourage those who seek for a larger unity within the incompleted pilgrimage: Chaucer was at least conscious of an aesthetic principle generally neglected if not actually unrecognized by his age.

The earliest of Chaucer's major works, however, the *Book of the Duchess*, ascribed by general consensus to 1369-70, has been frequently criticized for lack of unity and proportion. R. K. Root, for example, says:

It is as a work of the poet's youth ... that the *Book of the Duchess* deserves attention. Intrinsically its value is but slight. It is not lacking in beautiful and effective passages: but, taken as a whole, it furnishes but weary reading. ... The Ceyx and Alcyone story has so slight a

connection with the main theme of the poem that it constitutes a
serious breach of artistic unity. . . . But it is not till the lonely knight
begins to speak that the poem sinks to its true level of mediocrity.
Not only are his speeches intolerably long, they are also essentially
artificial. If he may be forgiven his conventional diatribe against
malicious fortune, and his strange conceit of the game of chess,
features borrowed from Machault, it is hard to overlook his uninter-
mitted pedantry. He ransacks the treasure-house of classical antiquity,
and the Bible as well, to furnish forth fit comparisons for his loss,
and, not content with this, stops now and then to explain a more
recondite allusion. . . .[3]

Bertrand Bronson has convincingly refuted at least part of this
charge by his sensitive and perceptive analysis of the elegy.[4] He
points out that the retelling of Ovid's tale of the drowned king of
Trachis enables Chaucer to state, through the words of Ceyx to
his bereft queen, the "human lesson" which upholds "resigned
acceptance" of the death of a loved one, and which the poet
cannot without presumption offer directly to his patron, John of
Gaunt. Both this passage (201-11) – and one might add that
Chaucer has deliberately made it the climax of his version of the
story, as it is not in Ovid, by the simple process of eliminating
some fifty lines devoted to the aftermath of Alcyone's dream in
the *Metamorphoses* – and the dreamer's earlier matter-of-fact
acceptance of his own sorrow ("but that is don./ Passe we over
untill eft", 40-1) introduce the consolation which the Black Knight
later needs ("For in your sorwe there lyth no red", 203) – a
consolation which, one might also add, is implied by the dreamer's final method, be it conscious or ingenuous, of forcing the
Knight to admit twice the stark reality of his lady's death. In
Mr. Bronson's words, "the true conclusion has been thrown forward from the end to an inconspicuous point where it can insinuate its meaning unobtrusively".[5]

If this interpretation has the validity which Professor Bronson's
persuasiveness encourages one to find, then Chaucer's method of

[3] Robert Kilburn Root, *The Poetry of Chaucer* (New York, 1906), pp.
60-1.
[4] Bertrand H. Bronson, "*The Book of the Duchess* Re-opened", *PMLA*,
LXVII (1952), 863-81.
[5] *Ibid.*, p. 881.

handling the classical story in relation to the dreamer's own distress reveals a touch of the irony which later dominates his work. Overwhelmed by an unrequited love of eight years' standing, the dreamer so suffers from sleeplessness that he fears he will die. Then, one night, rather "then play either at ches or tables", he whiles away the time by reading the story which concludes with Ceyx's message of resignation. The tale ended, the dreamer comments directly upon the consolation and help it affords to the distressed:

> For thus moche dar I saye wel,
> I had be dolven everydel,
> And ded, ryght thurgh defaute of slep
> Yif I ne had red and *take kep*
> Of this tale next before.
>
> (221-5)

Ironically, however, it is not Ceyx's climactic message to which the narrator refers, but rather the information which he has learned about Morpheus:

> For I had never herd speke, or tho,
> Of noo goddes that koude make
> Men to slepe, ne for to wake;
> For I ne knew never god but oon.
>
> (234-7)

In "game", he pledges to Morpheus, "Or hys goddesse, dame Juno/ Or som wight elles, I ne roghte who" (243-4) a feather bed and "many a pilowe" with pillowcases "of cloth of Reynes" in exchange for sleep; and no sooner has he completed his list of rather ridiculous though psychologically apt "fees" than he falls asleep to gain a rest which, we may assume, alleviates both the threat of death and his woe. The lightly humorous touch throughout this passage underscores the dreamer's literal-minded mis-interpretation of the thematic value of the Ovidian tale, for it is obviously not to suggest the bribing of pagan deities that Chaucer indirectly points out the desirability of taking "kep" of Ceyx and Alcyone. Although in the dreamer's case the reading of the tale promotes a sleep which forestalls death resulting from sorrow, if the message of the tale is properly applied, it may forestall sorrow resulting from a death. Thus, by having the dreamer state a truth which he immediately and ironically misapplies, Chaucer indicates the intimate relationship between the first and second parts of his elegy and emphasizes the paradoxical parallel between the dreamer and the Black Knight.

The continual emphasis upon death in the first half of the poem also ties it indirectly to the Knight's lament. Not only is the concept introduced literally by the dreamer's several assertions that unless he sleeps he will die, and by Alcyone's fears for Ceyx's fate, but a number of the relatively few figurative images also reiterate the theme. The dreamer declares "Defaute of slep and hevynesse/ Hath *sleyn* my spirit of quyknesse" (25-6); Alcyone swoons in a "*dede* slep" (127); the springs near Morpheus' cave make "a *dedly* slepynge soun" (162). In all, some sixteen references of one sort or another within the first 240 lines foreshadow the word which the Knight, as he talks to the dreamer, scrupulously avoids applying directly to his lady until the very end.

Similarly, the image of the physician who may heal sorrow which appears at the beginning of the poem, recurs significantly in the scene with the Knight. Originally, the figure is applied to the dreamer's misfortune:

> I holde hit be a sicknesse
> That I have suffred this eight yeer,
> And yet my boote is never the ner;
> For there is phisicien but oon
> That may me hele;
>
> (36-40)

Later, the dreamer expresses a sympathetic desire to make the Knight "hool" (553) and is told that "no physicien" may "hele" (571) the sorrow which the grief-shattered man endures. The overt progress of the poem, however, shows that the story of Ceyx and Alcyone leads the dreamer to a sleep which, if it does not "heal" his sorrow, at least provides some respite and may account for his "but that is don" attitude. By like token, the tale indirectly offers the same restorative to the bereaved husband of

Blanche of Lancaster, just as the dreamer's willing ear may be considered to provide a kind of purgative "boote" to the bereaved lover – "Paraunter hyt may ese youre herte" (556). Despite the denials incorporated into both uses of the image, a cure of sorts does exist for sorrow. That the dreamer found this respite by rejecting a game of chess provides yet another link between the first portion of the elegy and the latter, where the Knight describes his loss through the conceit of Fortune's checkmate.

Thus, it would seem that Chaucer wrote the *Book of the Duchess* with a very delicate awareness of the unified whole and that both irony and imagery play a part in the creation of that unity.[6] He does not develop irony through imagery here, as he later does in his fabliaux, but the two elements do function in a way significant to the overall structure of the poem.

Not all of the imagery in the elegy, however, is organic in the sense that the figures extend their significance beyond the direct point of comparison. Chaucer uses a number of similes which, although perfectly adequate for their immediate descriptive effect, not only are purely conventional but also function exclusively in terms of the surface appropriateness demanded by the writers of medieval poetics. Alcyone falls in a swoon "as cold as ston" (123); Morpheus' cave is "as derk/ As helle-pit" (170-1); the birds welcoming the May dawn sing a song as sweet as "hyt had be a thyng of heven" (308); there are seven times more flowers blooming in the green than "in the welken sterres bee" (409). When the Black Knight begins his lament, he compares Fortune's deceitfulness to that of a scorpion (636-41); he sees his lady in a crowd of ten thousand as "chef myrour of al the feste" (974); without her any company is "as a corowne withoute stones" (980); and so on.

Equally conventional, as many commentators have noted, is the extended portrait of the lady. In this passage, whether it be

---

[6] The dubious reader may object to this conclusion upon the grounds that many of Chaucer's details can be traced to Machaut and Froissart. (See Robinson's notes for instances.) Indisputable as this fact may be, Chaucer nonetheless chose only such details and took only such cues as he wanted, and the point of real significance is what he makes his borrowings do in their new context.

based upon Machaut [7] or merely upon the rhetorical tradition which the French poet was also following, Chaucer divides his description more or less into two parts, lines 855-960 being an *effictio* or enumeration of physical details, and lines 961-1033 a *notatio* or description of character. The former is considerably longer than the examples of the device given in the rhetorical-poetic treatises because the Knight also includes his own reactions to the lady's various beauties as well as a few comments which tend toward the *notatio*. He follows the formulaic pattern, however, describing first her hair "lyk gold", then her eyes "of good mochel, noght to wyde", her visage "whit, rody, fressh, and lyvely hewed", her voice "goodly, softe", and "swete", her neck "a round tour of yvoyre/ Of good gretnesse, and noghte to gret", and so on down to the modest conclusion of unseen beauties:

> Ryght faire shuldres and body long
> She had, and armes, every lyth
> Fattyssh, flesshy, not gret therwith;
> Ryght white handes, and nayles rede,
> Rounde brestes; and of good brede
> Hyr hippes were, a streight flat bak.
> I knew on hir noon other lak
> That all hir lymmes nere pure sewynge
> In as fer as I had knowynge.
>
> (952-60)

This is, of course, the ideal medieval woman, corresponding detail by detail to the concepts of personal beauty expressed by a vast variety of medieval writers. Walter Clyde Curry's study of this subject provides readily accessible verification on every point, but a few examples will suffice. He writes: "The type of hair most highly appreciated ... is what we would probably call the blonde. ... *Yellow* as gold is a common comparison used to intensify the charm of the color as well as to give some idea of the lustre of beautiful hair. ... Large, round, and wide-open eyes are an especial mark of beauty. ... Exceedingly large eyes, how-

---

[7] Harrison, "Med. Rhet. in *Book of the Duchess*", pp. 428-42, disagrees with Manly's statement that the portrait is a "free paraphrase" of lines 563-97 of the *Poetria Nova* (*C. and the Rhet.*, p. 103) and offers instead as a model the faithless lady in Machaut's *Le Jugement dou Roy de Behaingne*. His article cites all three parallel passages.

ever, are considered very ugly. . . . The skin of beautiful women and children must be . . . above all shining white. . . . The cheeks of both men and women, to be beautiful, must not be pale and wan, but fresh and well-colored. . . . Such cheeks or faces are sometimes said to be "ruddy". . . . In shape the neck of a beautiful woman should be small, round, so long as to be compared to that of a swan, or so plump that no bone may be seen. . . . The skin of the neck should be of . . . transparent whiteness. . . .' [8]

Such reliance upon convention not only for form of expression but also for total subject matter may, no doubt, be called "essentially artificial"; yet, oddly enough, Mr. Root excludes the description of Blanche from his rather harsh condemnation of the Knight's speeches and speaks praisingly of its portrayal of "noble womanhood". [9] However unsympathetic a modern reader may be, he finds it hard to deny that Chaucer has managed to make the commonplace ideal seem somehow real and the tribute movingly sincere. This result may stem from the Knight's interjection of his own enraptured reactions to first one and then another aspect of his lady's beauty combined with the reader's knowledge that she is dead. Nonetheless, the portrait is as purely rhetorical as the numerous brief *exempla* "ransacked from from the treasure-house of classical antiquity and the Bible" and as completely conventional as the protest against Fortune and the depiction of the Knight's love affair within the pattern of courtly love.

By the time Chaucer turned his attentions to the General Prologue of the *Canterbury Tales*, his handling of the portrait, as we all know, had undergone considerable modification. So much has been written upon the artistry and effectiveness of these sketches [10] that we may limit the discussion here to two points

---

[8]   Walter Clyde Curry, *The Middle English Ideal of Personal Beauty; as Found in the Metrical Romances, Chronicles, and Legends of the XIII, XIV, and XV Centuries* (Baltimore, 1916), pp. 12-13; 61; 80; 91; 99-101. See also pp. 71-2; 112; 113; 114; 121; 122-3.

[9]   Root (note 3), p. 63.

[10]   For typical discussions, see: Root (note 3), pp. 161-2; Emile Legouis, *Geoffrey Chaucer* (Blond, 1910), pp. 217-27; Lowes, *Geoffrey Chaucer*, pp. 198-203; J. R. Hulbert, "Chaucer's Pilgrims", *PMLA*, LXIV (1949), 823-8; E. T. Donaldson, ed., *Chaucer's Poetry* (New York, 1958), pp. 874-900; Muriel Bowden, *A Commentary on the General Prologue to the Canter-*

directly relevant to the concern of this study: first, the extent to which the depictions of the pilgrims differ from the prescriptions of the "rethors"; second, the use of irony within the portraits.

The *effictio* of Geoffrey of Vinsauf and Matthew of Vendôme, like its application in the *Roman de la Rose*, presents the ideal of an abstraction. Although one of their portraits may overtly describe Helen or Beroe, in essence it creates the epitome of beauty or of ugliness, just as the details selected by Guillaume de Lorris epitomize Hate, Villainy, Envy, and other allegorized concepts. The Canterbury pilgrims, by contrast, are representatives of actual human society; and yet, although Chaucer has turned from abstractions to the life of his times, the element of the ideal is still visible, for, as various critics have observed, all of the pilgrims are "champions". The Knight is a "verray, parfit gentil knyght", the Friar is the "beste beggere in his hous", there is "nowher so bisy a man" as the Sergeant of the Law, the Shipman has no peer "from Hulle to Cartage", the Miller always wins at "wrast-lynge", the Wife of Bath's skill in cloth-making surpasses "hem of Ypres and of Gaunt", and so on through a great diversity of nonpareils. Moreover, despite all the seemingly realistic and individualizing details included in a number of the portraits, the results are perfect examples of particular kinds of people, ranging from the near-saint to the most blatant sinner with a wide variety of intermediate shadings. Because the figures are drawn from the complexities of human personality, they cannot, however, in most cases, be summed up by a simple generic label; and the details which convey their quintessence do not come from pre-determined and widely accepted standards but rather from the poet's keen observation of human life. He recreates for us a figure recognizable as the epitome of things we also have observed about human behavior but have not reduced into a formulaic generalization.

Chaucer's process in depicting these paragons also differs markedly from the medieval theorists' models. In all but two of the portraits he intermingles the *effictio* and the *notatio*, the two exceptions being the descriptions of the Parson and the Manciple, which contain no visual details. The portraits of the Knight, the Clerk, the Man of Law, the Physician, and the Plowman are predominately *notatio*, but each includes at least one visual detail which reinforces the impression given by the presentation of character and abilities. Only the Yeoman is described primarily in terms of physical appearance, and here it is evident that Chaucer has abandoned the head-to-foot pattern of the traditional *effictio*. We see first the Yeoman's coat and hood, then the sheaf of arrows under his belt and the bow in his hand; from this we move to the place where the traditional *effictio* would begin, his "not heed . . . with a broun visage", then back to the guard on his arm, the sword by one side, the dagger on the other, and come finally to the St. Christopher medal on his chest and the horn which he carries. This same disordering of detail [11] is evident in the portraits in which the visual is interspersed with the *notatio*. In the case of the Wife of Bath, for example, we see first her red hose and supple shoes, and then her bold red face; after hearing about her husbands and her pilgrimages, we learn that she is gat-toothed and rides upon an "amblere", and then see her head-dress, her broad hips, and finally her spurs. In some instances it is possible to discern an underlying reason for the order chosen. The Wife's red hose and bold face appropriately introduce her amazing matrimonial career, just as the description of her hips and the pair of sharp spurs on her feet lead suggestively to the final statement that she knows all about the "olde daunce" of love; and the assertion that she is gat-toothed, which by her own interpretation (*W. of B. Pro.*, 603) reveals her Venerian nature, is so placed as to cast a deliberate sexual ambiguity upon the line which concludes the discussion of her many pilgrimages:

> She koude muchel of wandrynge by the weye.
> Gat-tothed was she, soothly for to seye.
>
> (467-8)

This sort of thematic relevance for the order of the details, however, is by no means omnipresent, and we may assume that

---

[11] This point has been considered at some length by Ralph Baldwin, "Unity of the Canterbury Tales", pp. 37-52.

Chaucer often has no other motive for his arrangement than the achievement of informality.

Unlike either the traditional *effictio* or *notatio*, the details in Chaucer's portraits are specific and unique. Where the conventional *notatio* expounds upon a person's character through abundant generalization, Chaucer tells us something specific about a pilgrim's habitual actions from which we may deduce his nature. Where the conventional *effictio* draws from widely accepted notions of what is beautiful and what is ugly, Chaucer selects visual details which suggest the essence of the pilgrim's personality: the Monk's face that shines "as he hadde been enoynt", the Knight's "gypon/ Al bismotered with his habergeon", the Miller's wart and nostrils "blake and wyde". It is, of course, within this aspect of the portraits that Chaucer's *ignis ingenii* becomes most apparent.

A second point of interest here about the portraits is their use of irony. Earle Birney, when incisively disputing the idea that Chaucer's characteristic irony emerged only after his introduction to Italian writers, has claimed that the poet might equally well have learned the "tricks" of ironic statement from medieval rhetorical-poetic doctrine. He writes:

Medieval rhetoric in fact recognized officially the curious value of saying something different from what is meant, not to deceive with a lie but to awaken to a truth. This effect, which is now likely to be called irony, gave the savor to such formal literary dishes as the *circumlocutio* and the *conduplicatio* (in amplification), and the *prosecutio con proverbiis*. Irony hovered around such recommended styles as the *humilis* and the *aenigma (stilus ornatus difficilis)* and occasionally even about the *sententia, dubitatio,* and *diminutio (ornatus facilis)*. Such tricks Chaucer could have learned as an esquire pursuing the obligatory *ars versificandi.*[12]

Examination of the texts of the medieval theorists, however, reveals that only in a most general way can these assertions be considered true. With the exception of *conduplicatio*,[13] the figures

[12] Earle Birney, "The Beginnings of Chaucer's Irony", *PMLA*, LIV (1939), 638.

[13] *Conduplicatio* in both the *ad Herennium* and the *Poetria Nova* is simply repetition of one or more words: "Conduplicatio est cum ratione amplificationis aut commiserationis eiusdem unius aut plurium verborum iteratio, hoc modo: '*Tumultus*, Gai Gracce, *tumultus* domesticos et intestinos conparas!'" (*ad Herennium*, IV, xxviii). I fail to see in what way

mentioned above do indeed involve saying something other than one's direct meaning, but the "rethors" do not suggest that the process includes the element of oppositeness requisite to irony, nor do they ever imply that the figures are ways to "awaken to a truth".[14] Of circumlocution, for example, Geoffrey says:

Est gradus ulterior quando, quia transilit aures
Dictio, vox curta, fit sermo vicarius ejus
In serie vocum longa serieque morosa.
Longius ut sit opus, ne ponas nomina rerum:
Pone notas alias; nec plane detege, sed rem
Innue per notulas; nec sermo perambulet in re,
Sed rem circuiens longis ambagibus ambi
Quod breviter dicturus eras, et tempora tardes . . .
                         (*Poetria Nova*, 226-33)

[A further step is (since speech cut short springs right past the ears) to make discourse in a long and obstinate series of words substitute for the terse expression. So that the work may be longer, you do not put down the mere names of things; use other words; do not lay a thing completely bare but insinuate it by little signs; do not let the discourse pass through a thing, but walk round about with lengthy circumlocutions the thing which you were about to utter more briefly and you draw out the time . . .]

In using circumlocution, of course, a particular poet might select phrases which would be ironic but Geoffrey's precepts do not suggest this as a possibility. He, in fact, seems concerned here merely with emphasis. The trope from the *ad Herennium* called *permutatio*, however, does involve ironic statement. Geoffrey discusses this figure as an example of "transsumptio" without actually defining the term, but the illustrations which he gives make it clear that he understood the concept as nothing more than derisive misnomer:

                    vel transfero nomen
Ex alia causa, ne sit similatio vera,
Immo per antifrasim, tanquam derisio, quando
Corpore deformem *Paridem*, vel corde ferocem
Aeneam, vel vi fragilem cognomino *Pirrum*,
Aut sermone rudem *Ciceronem*, vel petulantem
Ypolitum.
                         (*Poetria Nova*, 929-35)

Mr. Birney finds this ironic; nor does there seem to be any more justification for his claim of irony in the style *humilis* (see pp. 36-8 *supra*).
[14] See Faral, pp. 117, 204, 233, 347, 355.

[or I transfer a noun for another reason, not so that the likeness may be true, nay rather as if I were deriding through antiphrasis, as when I call a person deformed in body "Paris", or savage of heart "Aeneas", or feeble in strength "Pyrrhus", or petulant "Hypolitus".]

Both the limitations in the irony to be achieved with *permutatio* and its doubtful presence, as far as the theorists are concerned, in the figures advanced by Mr. Birney suggest that Chaucer's peculiar kind of irony really owes little to medieval rhetorical-poetic precept. It is far more accurate to say that Chaucer often invests the *sententia* (maxim), the *dubitatio* (feigned hesitation) and the *diminutio* (disparagement of self) with irony, and although he is perhaps no more unique in this practice than he is in his ironic point of view toward life, the very pervasiveness of his irony in all of its various manifestations implies that it stems from an aspect of his peculiar sensibility rather than from literary model. This is not to say, of course, that his taste for the ironic was not nourished by his knowledge of other ironists [15] – his favorite Latin author, after all, was Ovid.

[15] Earle Birney (note 13), pp. 638-9, points out that many literary sources exist which might have stimulated Chaucer's taste for the ironic. In another article – "English Irony Before Chaucer", *University of Toronto Quarterly*, VI (1937), 538-57 – he summarizes his investigations along these lines as follows: "Chaucer, being Chaucer, had little to learn from these rare grim jests of Langland, nor can we be sure that he went to school to any one ironist, English or continental; but he could scarcely escape the influence of this long tradition of ironic speech in the language and literature of his own country. No one has rightly savoured the great ironies of the *Prologue to the Canterbury Tales* if he has not also tasted the coltish wit of Gamelyn, or the elaborately guarded assaults of the political ballad-mongers, or the *saeva indignatio* of Bromyard and Wiclif. Even the Italianate *Troilus* can be better understood if we catch echoes, behind its perfect cadences, of those mournful overtones of Fate in the *Anglo-Saxon Chronicle*, or of Hendyng's wry and slangy wisdom.

"There are, of course, still more important ancestral ghosts of Chaucer's irony to be conjured from other literature – the Latin and Italian and French worthies whose names we have been compelled to hurry over, or to leave unmentioned. There are the anecdotal elegances of Ovid and Appolinarus Sidonus and Ekkehard IV, and of John of Bridlington and Jean de Hauteville; the ironies, tragic and comic, of the Vulgate; the edged praises of Dante for his birthplace, Florence; the subtle malices of Jean de Meun and Jean de Condé and Deschamps; the dramatic intricacies of the French fabliaux; and the wit of that greatest and most delightful treasury of all medieval irony, the multiple saga of Reynard the Fox" (pp. 556-7).

Whatever may be the source of Chaucer's irony, there is no question about the fact that he spices the General Prologue with it liberally. He ranges from the delightful but obvious device of having himself as pilgrim approve of the wrong things – "And I seyde his opinion was good" (183) in reference to the Monk's rejection of monastic seclusion, for example – to the subtle suggestion of flaw in the Prioress through details which are overtly commendatory.[16] In this latter case, the irony actually results from the imagery – the courtly manners, the fluted wimple, the "fetys" cloak, the gold brooch all suggesting a slight feminine affectation not precisely fitting for a nun, the pet dogs and the uncovered forehead implying some laxity in religious discipline. Thus, we have here an example of the union of irony and imagery which Chaucer develops into a clearly defined technique in some of his individual tales, and in a number of the other more clearly satiric portraits various visual details augment the irony created by the narrator's naive enthusiasm.

In addition to this sort of merging of the two elements, the Prologue also furnishes examples of irony arising from figurative comparison. Of the Monk, for example, Chaucer writes:

> A manly man, to been an abbot able.
> Ful many a deyntee hors hadde he in stable,
> And whan he rood, men myghte his brydel heere
> Gynglen in a whistlynge wynd als cleer
> And eek as loude *as dooth the chapel belle.*
>
> (167-171)

The "chapel belle", of course, immediately suggests what a devout monk ought to be hearing and implies the whole deviation from monastic life which the pilgrim's later views on Augustinian rule make explicit and which hardly qualifies him as a suitable candidate for abbot. Similarly, the religious connotations associated

[16] The ambiguities of the Prioress' portrait have been so frequently discussed as to require no documented reiteration here. Typical examples of lucid commentary on the subject are: John Livingstone Lowes, "Simple and Coy", *Anglia*, XXXIII (1910), 440-51; John M. Steadman, "The Prioress' Dogs and Benedictine Discipline", *Modern Philology*, LIV (1956), 1-6; H. S. Bennett, "Medieval Literature and the Modern Reader", *Essays and Studies*, XXXI (1945), 9-11; Bowden (note 10), pp. 92-104.

with annointment ironically suggest the same basic discrepancy
when the Monk's well-fed face is described as shining as if "he
hadde been enoynt" (199). In the portrait of the Friar, Chaucer
uses a metaphor which seems to have the kind of ironic but vulgar
double-entendre evident in a number of his fabliaux. He calls the
Friar a "noble post" unto his order, thus creating a verbal echo
of the now-commonplace "pillar of the church"; yet, the context
in which he places this phrase, directly after the covert reference
to the Friar's numerous seductions, so completely denies any
justification for the praise that the metaphor almost of necessity
also becomes phallic:

> In alle the ordres foure is noon that kan
> So muchel of daliaunce and fair langage.
> He hadde maad ful many a mariage
> Of yonge wommen at his owene cost.
> Unto his ordre he was a noble post.
>
> (210-14)

Chaucer also occasionally uses details in the portraits which re-
appear ironically in the tales told by the pilgrims, and thus he
creates yet another sort of ironic significance for his imagery.
Perhaps the clearest example of this process appears in the portraits of the Friar and the Summoner. The Friar tells his story to
insult his professional rival, and with unerring instinct he describes a fictitious summoner who lasciviously spies out sexual
irregularities in order that he may collect money for not reporting
the offenses. Thus, he exposes characteristics of his fellow pilgrim, who, we learn from his portrait in the General Prologue, is
also lecherous (626; 663-5) and eager to accept bribes (649-57).
Ironically, however, details in the Friar's portrait reveal that he,
too, is lecherous (211-13) and is willing to take bribes instead of
strictly adhering to his religious duties (221-32); and with a
masterstroke, Chaucer makes the ironic parallel between the rival
rascals explicit and clear-cut by one specific word:

> For thogh a *wydwe* hadde noght a sho
> So plesaunt was his "In principio",
> Yet wolde he have a ferthyng, er he wente.
>
> (253-5)

In the Friar's tale, of course, it is the summoner's attempted extortion from a WIDOW which brings about his downfall. Similarly, when the Summoner retorts with his crude tale about a friar, he endows his protagonist with a characteristic which the Prologue tells us is his own: the quoting of bits of Church Latin (637-46). This ironic touch of unwitting self-revelation in two tales dramatically inspired to expose the moral inadequacies of rival professions reasserts the essential likeness of the two pilgrims and explicitly points out that the attempt of each to denigrate the other is clearly a case of the pot calling the kettle black.

The portraits of the pilgrims, then, illustrate Chaucer's creation of irony through imagery and his adaptation of a stylized rhetorical-poetic device to suit his own purposes. When these two traits are united with the extended significance for figurative comparisons and the awareness of the unified whole evident in the *Book of the Duchess*, they form the technique which Chaucer uses in handling the imagery of his fabliaux. And this technique, as J. V. Cunningham has said about the portraits of the pilgrims, is "both original and traditional at the same time".[17]

---

[17]   J. V. Cunningham, "The Literary Form of the Prologue to the *Canterbury Tales*", *Modern Philology*, XLIX (1952), 181.

IV

THE FRIAR'S TALE

Nevill Coghill once remarked that the *Friar's Tale* is "a piece in Chaucer's maturest vein of bland anecdote, and shows what a master can do with a chestnut" [1] If one may be allowed a facetious application of rhetorical terminology, this statement partakes of litotes more than hyperbole. Indeed, the Friar's story, because of its brevity and relative simplicity, illustrates perhaps more clearly than all other tales the transcendent quality of Chaucer's art. The poet takes an old popular plot, decks it out in completely conventional rhetorical-poetic devices, incorporates sufficient "auctoritees" to delight the medieval ear, and directs the whole to a traditional medieval moral purpose. Yet, the result is a miniature masterpiece which is as unique as it is conventional.

Although no immediate source for Chaucer's tale has been found, the generic story pejoratively labelled a "chestnut" was a commonplace medieval anecdote of the simplest sort and one which has survived in various forms in jestbooks and collections of *exempla*.[2] These consistently brief, straight-forward, artless narratives were apparently modified at will to make them apply to any unpopular official; [3] thus, in adapting the story of the heart-felt curse for the Friar of the *Canterbury Tales* to tell as an insult to his professional rival, the Summoner, Chaucer was merely following the practice of popular tradition.

[1] Nevill Coghill, *The Poet Chaucer* (Oxford, 1949), p. 162.
[2] See: Robert Dudley French, *A Chaucer Handbook* (New York, 1947), pp. 284-7; Archer Taylor, "The Devil and the Advocate", *PMLA*, XXXVI (1921), 269-74; William Frank Bryan and Germaine Dempster, *Sources and Analogues of Chaucer's Canterbury Tales* (Chicago, 1941), pp. 269-74.
[3] French (note 2), p. 284.

The effectiveness of the numerous analogues depends entirely upon the irony implicit in a situation whereby a would-be victimizer becomes himself the victim of a devil, and in its simplest outlines the *Friar's Tale* is no exception. An unscrupulous summoner sets out to extort money from a poor widow, and on the way he meets a stranger with whom he swears an oath of brotherhood. After the latter has boasted of being a devil, the two encounter an enraged carter condemning his team of horses to hell, but when the summoner suggests that his friend take the property thus given him, the other replies that he cannot do so because the curses are not sincere. Immediately thereafter, the summoner affronts the widow who is the object of his designs. She consigns him to the devil with utter sincerity, and the friend, who proves indeed to be what he had boasted, snatches his booty and carries the summoner off to hell.

To this stark skeleton, however, Chaucer adds realistic characterization, disclosed in part by typical portrait description but primarily by self-revealing speech and action, and he vitalizes the situation with a subtle dramatic conflict between the protagonists which emerges through the ironic implications of the dialogue and gains intensity and comic force through varied levels of awareness. Furthermore, he builds a pattern of images which parallels the action of the tale and reinforces and deepens the comic irony both inherent and explicit within it. This pattern emphasizes the movement of the narrative, clarifies the intention, foreshadows the outcome, and, as a result of all these functions, tightens the artistic unity of the whole. The scope of Chaucer's contribution to the popular anecdote in this regard is suggested by the fact that none of the analogues contains imagery of any sort other than such a stale metaphor as "from the bottom of his heart".[4] Chaucer's images are almost equally commonplace and conventional; yet, he so manipulates them that they serve an organic function within the aesthetic whole of the tale, and thus he transcends the traditional even as he adheres to its essential forms.

[4]   *Ibid.*, p. 286; Bryan and Dempster, p. 271, cites an analogue from the *Promptuarium exemplorum*, which includes the line: "Ecce, isti dederunt te mihi *ex intimo corde*, et ideo meus es."

It is significant not only that ALL the metaphors and similes in the *Friar's Tale* contribute to a dominant image but also that this image is the only one in the narrative: all the formal figures of speech depict various kinds of hunters and their prey.[5] Although these comparisons are dispersed economically throughout the first half of the tale, their interweaving lines gradually form a pattern, and this single, emphatically consistent image is obviously intended to serve some function. Even if its use were determined by mere appropriateness or decorum, the result would be a kind of thematic imagery which goes far beyond any of the functions implied for imagery by the medieval writers of poetics.

The first seventy-five lines of the *Friar's Tale* are devoted to *notatio* describing the sly, money-loving summoner and his harsh, equally greedy employer, the archdeacon. Within this passage the summoner is first compared to a hare:

> For thogh this somonour *wood were as an hare*,
> To telle his harlotrye I wol nat spare.
>
> **(1327-8)**[6]

The expression "as mad as a March hare" is so common a proverbial saying [7] that it probably evokes no visual image any more than does the phrase "from the bottom of his heart", and hence the significance of the comparison here is not immediately discerned. However, it illustrates Chaucer's method of twisting the commonplace or traditional to suit his own purposes, for the

---

[5] Even the initial description of a bishop's hauling in sinners with his crosier ("For er the bisshop caughte hem with his hook,/ They weren in the erchedeknes book", 1317-18), which Adrien Bonjour has called a "deliciously irreverent image" ("Aspects of Chaucer's Irony in 'The Friar's Tale' ", *Essays in Criticism*, XI (1961), 122), and which is essentially extraneous to the tale of the two protagonists except in so far as it helps to set the tone of the introduction, corresponds to the basic theme: in this visual distortion of the crosier, the bishop as hunter captures his prey.

[6] In line 1327 I have changed Robinson's capitalization of the word "somonour" to lower case because, as I have argued elsewhere ("An Ambiguous Reference in Chaucer's *Friar's Tale*", *Archiv*, CXCVIII (1962), 388-90), Chaucer intends the word to refer to the protagonist of the tale rather than to the Friar's rival, the pilgrim. In capitalizing the name so that it designates the pilgrim, Mr. Robinson has departed from both the major MSS, and the practice of previous editors.

[7] W. W. Skeat, *Early English Proverbs* (Oxford, 1910), p. 115.

subsequent narrative shows that he intends to associate with his central character both the idea of the hare as an animal preyed upon by men and birds alike and the concept of madness.

A few lines later the Friar says that the summoner had "bawdes redy to his hond,/ As any *hauk* to lure in Engelond" (1339-40) and goes on to add that he could spot a lecher better than any "*dogge* for the bowe/ That kan an *hurt deer* from an hool yknowe" (1369-70). Then the action of the narrative begins:

> And so bifel that ones on a day
> This somnour, *evere waityng on his pray*,
> Rood for to somne an old wydwe, a ribibe,
> Feynynge a cause, for he wolde brybe.
>
> (1375-8)

By this point the image cluster has begun to take significant shape. The protagonist is pictured as a hunter preying on his victims, innocent and guilty alike, with the ruthlessness of the hawk and the avidness of the dog after the wounded deer. The concept thus established is reinforced with yet another simile: "This somonour . . . was as ful of jangles/ As ful of venym been thise *waryangles*" (1407-8). The summoner's talkativeness is the point of immediate reference, but like the hawk, the waryangle (the modern shrike) is also a bird of prey. And yet, paradoxically, although the summoner is the predatory pursuer, he is simultaneously the "wood hare", the frequent victim of hunters and just such birds as the hawk.

The ironic import of this double image foreshadows the events which are about to occur, for while the summoner is in pursuit of his victim, the widow, he becomes himself the object of a far more effective hunter, the devil. Considering that Chaucer's final comparison of the summoner to a shrike occurs after the devil has been introduced, one may even venture the argument that it deliberately points up the contrast between the powers of the two hunters: although most varieties of shrikes prey upon mere insects which they impale upon thorns, the devil's victim is man himself. The foreshadowing function of this paradoxical image is not likely to have escaped Chaucer's audience, for in the midst of the description which contains the figures of speech discussed above, the Friar also alludes to Judas, who damned himself for money:

> And right as Judas hadde purses smale,
> And was a theef, right swich a theef was he; [the summoner]
>   (1350-1)

In an age so thoroughly imbued in Biblical tradition as was the fourteenth century, this reference must surely have prompted the listeners to expect signs of a similar fate for the avaricious summoner.

Thus, the composite image which has just emerged allows us to realize the irony inherent in the tale, for it permits us to share from the beginning the poet's understanding of a situation which the character vitally concerned comprehends only at the last. While the summoner erroneously looks upon himself only as hunter and acts in a manner naturally and logically suited to his role as he perceives it, we see him more accurately as both hunter and prey. Nor is Chaucer's use of the epithet "wood" accidental, for once the action of the story is underway, the summoner reveals his heedlessness and stupidity – indeed, his madness – by completely disregarding the most obvious warnings of his impending fate. He entraps himself unwittingly. His complete unscrupulousness, his greed, his hypocrisy, and, above all, his stupidity and his pride in his own supposed cleverness lead him to seal his own doom. He condemns himself; he attempts to deceive the arch-deceiver. In the subsequent events we can recognize the dramatic conflict between the two characters and can appreciate the full depth of the irony because we have been given an insight which allows us to view the action on two distinct levels.

The ironic complexity of the situation increases with the entrance of the devil. Through a traditional *effictio* Chaucer expands his basic image to include the second hunter tacitly demanded by the double role previously established for the summoner. Like the Knight's Yeman in the General Prologue, the fiend wears a green coat and carries a bow and "arwes brighte and kene" (1381), and the summoner naturally assumes from this garb that the stranger is a yeoman. We, however, being as it were in the poet's confidence, can perceive the intricate irony of this disastrous mistake of identity. Because green clothing is traditional for underworld spirits who walk the earth,[8] and because the figure of the hunting devil is equally traditional,[9] the stranger's very first appearance gives us a clue to his own true nature. At the same time we realize that the summoner's assumption is correct, but in a way which he does not suspect, for the devil actually IS a hunter – a hunter, moreover, who has just flushed his prey!

Considered thus, the irony of the situation is further deepened by the summoner's vain attempt to deceive the devil in precisely the same way that he himself is deceived. The unsuspecting victim lies about his profession, pretending to be a bailiff, for he "dorste nat, for verray filthe and shame/ Seye that he was a somonour" (1393-4), and the fiend replies, "Depardieux . . . deere broother,/ Thou art a bailly, and I am another" (1395-6). This loaded statement contains three levels of meaning, only one of which, of course, is evident to the victim: in addition to the overt assertion, the line implies that the devil is no more a bailiff than is the summoner; even more subtle is the truth of his remark, for the duties he has come to perform ARE those of a bailiff – to administer justice and collect his lord's due, in this case the soul of this "false theef".

The summoner, however, cannot hide his true nature for long. When the devil offers to share his gold and silver if the summoner should happen to visit his shire, the latter immediately takes a pledge of brotherhood. Unknowingly, he allows his greed to lead him into what we recognize as a trap set for the "wood hare". Unaware of how transparent his interest is, he questions his new "brother" about the location of his home, but the double meaning of the devil's reply is apparent only to us:

> "Brother . . . fer in the north contree,
> Where-as I hope som tyme I shal thee see.

---

[8]   Robert Max Garrett, "The Lay of Sir Gawayne and the Green Knight", *JEGP*, XXIV (1925), 129; Curry, *Ideal of Personal Beauty*, p. 50; J. R. Hulbert, "Sir Gawayn and the Grene Kny3t", *Modern Philology*, XIII (1915), 454-60; D. W. Robertson, "Why the Devil Wears Green", *Modern Language Notes*, LXIX (1954), 470-2.

[9]   See Przemyslaw Mroczkowski, " 'The Friar's Tale' and its Pulpit Background", *English Studies Today*, 2nd series (1961), 111.

Er we departe, I shal thee so well wisse
That of myn hous ne shaltow nevere mysse."

(1413-16)

The summoner fails to realize the significance of the "north
contree", which is associated with infernal regions in Biblical
tradition and Germanic mythology,[10] and his blindness to the
devil's purpose prevents him from seeing that he has almost no
chance, indeed, of missing the "hous". In fact, he now insures
the doom which we anticipate, for he falls for a trick which
brings him to an open confession of his misdeeds. When he
questions the infernal "bailiff" about his technique for gaining
profit from his office, the latter describes exactly such unscrupulous practices as the summoner habitually uses. As a result, the
summoner forgets his assumed respectability and exclaims:

"Now certes . . . so fare I.
I spare nat to taken, God it woot,
But if it be to hevy or to hoot.
What I may gete in conseil prively,
No maner conscience of that have I.
Nere myn extorcioun, I mighte nat lyven,
Ne of swiche japes wol I nat be shryven.
Stomak ne conscience ne knowe I noon;
I shrewe thise shrifte-fadres everychoon.

(1434-42)

Thus, the devil's appeal to the summoner's greed has produced
precisely the desired effect; not only does the unsuspecting victim
voluntarily swear an oath which binds him to his destiny and
admit his own guilt, but he also abjures confession and penance,
the one source of forgiveness which might even yet save his soul.
In his delight at having found a boon companion who is apparently both rich and generous, he even cries out: "Wel be we
met, by God and by Seint Jame!" (1443). The comic irony of
his exclamation is apparent to us, for we know that if he understood the import of the encounter, he would hardly consider that
the two of them were "wel met". On yet another level, however,
the meeting, by God and by Saint James, is providential, for it

---

[10] See Robinson's note, p. 705, and Mroczkowski (note 9), p. 114.

gives the devil his opportunity to serve as "Goddes instrument" (1483) in ridding the world of an evil parasite, a function which he later explains to the heedless summoner.

Knowing the extent to which he can mislead his victim, the devil now begins to tell the truth quite outspokenly. Although he asserts that he is a "feend" whose "dwellyng is in helle" and indicates exactly what is to happen to his "brother deere", he does so in such a way that the summoner completely misses the point. Just before announcing his real identity, the devil begins "a litel for to smyle" (1446), and because we have been able to watch the preceding events unfold on different levels, we realize that the summoner's initial hypocrisy regarding his profession is now about to blind him to the openly stated truth. He notices the smile and assumes that his friend is lying, just as he has lied himself. The playful casualness of his reaction to the news indicates his fatal error:

> "A!" quod this somonour, "benedicite!" what sey ye?
> I wende ye were a yeman trewely.
>
> (1456-7)

Secure in his belief that he understands what is actually happening, he is willing to go along with what seems to him an amusing pretense. He asks several questions about hell and the nature of fiends, but he fails to catch the implications of the replies, which are full of Biblical and classical allusions. Take, for example, the devil's reference to Dante and Virgil:

> For thou shalt, by thyn owene experience,
> Konne in a chayer rede of this sentence
> Bet than Virgile, while he was on lyve,
> Or Dant also.
>
> (1517-20)

The illiterate summoner apparently does not know that these two poets are authorities on conditions in hell any more than he grasps the significance of such open warnings as the devil's remark that "A lowsy jogelour kan deceyve thee,/ And pardee, yet kan I moore craft than he" (1467-8). Even when his friend says, "brother myn, thy wit is al to bare/ To understonde" (1480-1), we may assume that the summoner thinks this statement merely an evasion of the question he has just asked, and he certainly makes no personal application of the devil's statement that if a victim "withstandeth oure temptacioun,/ It is a cause of his savacioun" (1497-8). The fiend also asserts that he would ride to the world's end for a "*preye*" (1455) and that devils will "swiche formes make" as best enable them "*preyes* for to take" (1471-2). To the victim such metaphors are but part of an elaborate lie which his "brother" is facetiously attempting to make him believe, but we, on the contrary, are reminded of the basic image which has allowed us to savor the full irony of this conversation and to see it as a dramatic conflict of character.

Some authoritative critics, such as Germaine Dempster and R. K. Root,[11] have based their interpretations of the tale upon the assumption that the summoner believes what the devil says about his true identity; they suggest that the summoner is so abject, his soul so hardened in crime, that he has no fear of pledging brotherhood with a fiend. Yet, Miss Dempster is not entirely at ease with this interpretation, for she admits that it "involves a sacrifice of realism to the requirements of satire, a rather un-Chaucerian feature which gives a very special, weird, and unreal coloring to the different episodes and their strokes of dramatic irony'.[12] The present argument, by contrast, makes Chaucer's intention more subtle, more deeply ironic, and indeed completely "Chaucerian". The man who prides himself upon the very thing which he lacks is a favorite character with Chaucer, as evidenced by old January or Absalom, the rustic adherent of courtly love in the *Miller's Tale* – to say nothing of the Pardoner, who delights in preaching in the grand style, however ludicrous his voice "as smal as hath a goot" must make his oratorical eloquence. If one considers that the summoner believes what the devil eventually tells him, then the whole central portion of the tale (1448-1522) becomes nothing more than a long learned digression on the nature of fiends, and the devil's sly remarks about deceiving the summoner have

[11] Germaine Dempster, *Dramatic Irony in Chaucer, Stanford University Publications*, IV, no. 3 (1932), 42-5; Root, *The Poetry of Chaucer*, pp. 248-9.
[12] Dempster (note 11), p. 42.

no apparent point. It is only if the summoner does NOT believe what he hears that the heart of the narrative becomes an intrinsic part of the whole, an ironic clash of character in which the overt deceiver craftily employs truth as a means of continuing the original deception. The validity of this interpretation is supported by the poet's own testimony in the image pattern as well as in what he has his characters say; and it is perhaps also significant that, although in some versions of the story the devil is recognized, the closest of the analogues states explicitly that the victim does not realize the identity of his companion.[13]

When the unutterably dense but realistic summoner reaffirms his brotherhood with the "feend", he says:

> I am a yeman, knowen is ful wyde;
> My trouthe wol I holde, as in this cas.
> For though thou were the devel Sathanas,
> My trouthe wol I holde to my brother,
> As I am sworn, and each of us til oother,
> For to be trewe brother in this cas . . .
>
> (1524-9)

The tone of his qualifying clause, "though thou were the devel Sathanas", is not clear, but the line certainly can be so read as to suggest "even though you claimed to be Satan himself", thereby implying the mistrust which the summoner's own dishonesty has fostered and indicating his acceptance of his friend's supposed game. The line which introduces this assertion is equally ambiguous, "I am a yeman, knowen is ful wyde", and although this may be taken as a satiric jibe at the constancy of men of higher rank, it is still an evasion of the summoner's true identity and claims a kind of integrity for the rascal which we have ample reason to doubt. Thus, he vainly attempts to keep up a disguise which he would surely consider unnecessary if he truly believed that he had sworn brotherhood with a devil rather than with a congenial (and wealthy) hypocrite who is practising the sum-

---

[13]   Bryan and Dempster, pp. 271-2. Even if readers prefer what is essentially a less amusing and less ironic interpretation of the summoner's character, the basic image pattern is no less significant, for the summoner, whatever his beliefs about his companion, certainly fails utterly to realize that he himself is the victim.

moner's own deceit. In similar fashion, his reaction when they meet the swearing carter reveals further his erroneous judgment of the devil's veracity. He says to himself, "Heere shal we have a pley" (1548) and then, drawing near the fiend (1549), proposes that the devil take the horses. With sly but useless cleverness, unaware of how tightly his blind assumptions have ensnared him in the nets of his own sins, he intends to use the situation to expose his long-winded, lying friend. In his obliviousness, he is indeed the "wood hare" to which he was first compared.

Up to this point much of the humor in the tale has resulted from an exact parallelism between the positions and actions of the two characters. The official function of each is to summon sinners to answer for offenses. When the two meet, each hides his identity under the same bailiff disguise; yet each later reveals his true nature, the summoner unconsciously, the devil artfully. In terms of the basic image each is a hunter who has found his prey, but the two victims, the summoner and the widow, remain unaware of the impending danger. The paradoxical image developed in the first hundred lines of the tale makes it possible for us to realize this parallelism as it unfolds and thus to appreciate the full measure of both the humor and the irony. In the final episode both hunters will descend simultaneously upon their preys, but only the stronger will emerge with the kill.

In this concluding scene, in which the summoner curses himself ("the foule feend me fecche/ if I th'excuse" – 1610-1) and so outrages the widow that she condemns him with heart-felt sincerity, the image of the "wood hare" gains an added implication. The original basis for the saying "mad as a March hare" was the observation that hares behave with erratic recklessness during the breeding season, traditionally the month of March.[14] So widely accepted was this concept at one time that the hare became a common symbol for lechery, and allegorical drawings frequently extolled the triumph of chastity by depicting a hare crushed beneath the feet of a maiden.[15] These associations of lechery and

14 Skeat (note 7).
15 Eug. Droulers, *Dictionnaire des Attributs, Allégories, Emblèmes et Symboles* (Turnhout, Belgium, 1948), p. 129. See also: E. P. Evans, *Animal Symbolism in Ecclesiastical Architecture* (New York, 1906), p. 228.

of heedlessness prompted by sex are ironically duplicated in the
summoner, who excels in extorting the gold he so loves from
accused adulterers. The introductory description has established
the fact that he employs bawds to spy out potential victims, and
in this concluding episode it is most apt that, by accusing the
widow of sexual trespass, he incites the curse which allows the
devil to seize him:

> ". . . Whan that thou madest thyn housbonde cokewold,
> I payde at hoom for thy correccioun."
>   "Thou lixt!" quod she, "by my savacioun,
> Ne was I nevere er now, wydwe ne wyf,
> Somoned unto youre court in al my lyf;
> Ne nevere I nas but of my body trewe!
> Unto the devel blak and rough of hewe
> Yeve I thy body and my panne also!"
>
> (1616-23)

Thus, the basic image gains further ironic intensity. Not only is
the summoner both hunter and prey, but he is also vulnerable to
destruction in the same manner as the "mad hare" and for
ironically similar reasons: his absorption in the profit to be extracted from sexual impulses, actual or pretended, makes him
recklessly oblivious to mortal danger. Moreover, although the
figures are vastly different, virtue here triumphs over the "hare"
even as it does in its graphic allegorical representations. With this
added complexity, the organic relationship of the composite
image to the over-all structure is strengthened, even as the image,
in turn, tightens the unity of the whole.

When at the end of the tale the Friar points out a moral for
the benefit of the listeners, he uses the same hunter-prey image
but diverts it from his characters to the pilgrims themselves. He
warns them to take heed of the summoner's fate, for although
this victim was guilty, "the temptour Sathanas", like the lion (a
traditional symbol for the devil) [16] "sit in his awayt alway/ To
sle the innocent, if that he may" (1657-8). But, he adds, if they
dispose their hearts to withstand the "feend", Christ will be their
"champion and knyght". In this way the image of the human

[16]   Evans (note 15), pp. 87-9.

prey is extended to include a defender who blends, in typical medieval fashion, the chivalric tradition with the Christian,[17] and the shift in application of the image turns Chaucer's masterpiece of comic irony into an exemplum which is at once completely in keeping with the traditions of his age and yet artistically unique.[18]

---

[17] Notable examples are the episodes of harrowing of hell in *Piers Plowman* and the section of the *Ancrene Wisse* usually entitled "The Love of Christ".

[18] In an article which came to my attention after the writing of this chapter, Earle Birney discusses the hunter-prey imagery of the tale; his conclusions about its ironic relationship to the narrative, however, differ considerably from my own. See: " 'After His Ymage': the Central Ironies of the 'Friar's Tale' ", *Mediaeval Studies*, XXI (1959), 17-35.

V

THE REEVE'S TALE

The *Reeve's Tale*, like the *Friar's Tale*, uses imagery to create an ironic parallel which tightens the unity of the action as a whole. Unlike the technique in the *Friar's Tale*, however, the parallel does not serve as counterpoint to the entire narrative; rather, it functions both to establish an essential relationship between the two scenes of subterfuge which make up the major part of the plot and to intensify and individualize the irony extant in the stereotyped situation of the trickster duped by his own gulls.

As Walter Morris Hart was the first to point out, the *Reeve's Tale* is more tightly integrated than its very similar analogue, the French fabliau *Le Meunier et les Deux Clers*, because Chaucer makes the "mainspring" of the whole tale the contest between the clerks and the miller.[1] John and Aleyn know that Symkin has succeeded in cheating them despite their determination to protect their grain, and their subsequent actions are dictated by a desire for revenge. In the fabliau the clerks do not suspect the theft, and the nighttime comedy of errors results merely from their libidinous urges. No one has commented upon the fact, however, that Chaucer also alters the details of the miller's trick. In the French poem the clerks arrive at the mill not with a stallion but with a mare which belongs to the brother of one of them:

> "Il nos est très bien avenu;
> Car j'ai un mien frere ensemant,
> Qui a une grasse *jumant*;

[1] Walter Morris Hart, "The Reeve's Tale: A Comparative Study of Chaucer's Narrative Art", *PMLA*, XXIII (1908), 9-17.

Je la prandrai, pran lo setier,
Et si devandron bolangier.

(A-text, 44-8)[2]

They put the sack of grain inside the mill, turn the mare loose in
a meadow, and while one clerk stays behind to keep an eye on
their two separated possessions, the other goes in search of the
miller:

Li clerc ont tost l'uis desfermé,
Si ont lo sac dedanz gité:
Après ont mis en un prael
La jumant, joste lo choisel.
Li uns remest por tot garder,
L'autre ala lo munier haster,
Que il les venist avancier.
Mais il s'an fu alé mucier:
Bien ot les clers veü venir,
Je cuit à aus voldra partir.

(61-70)

The miller's wife sends the first clerk on a wild goose chase into
the woods, the second soon goes after him, and the miller pops
out of hiding and steals both the bag and the horse.

Chaucer, by contrast, substitutes a stallion for the mare and
has Symkin effect a far more subtle trick which makes use of the
instinctive reactions of the horse. While the two clerks are scrupulously watching the grinding of their grain to forestall the thieving
miller, Symkin slips out of the mill and finds the stallion securely
tied in an arbor:

And to the hors he goth hym faire and wel;
He strepeth of the brydel right anon.
And whan the hors was loos, he gynneth gon
Toward the fen, ther wilde mares renne,
And forth with "wehee," thurgh thikke and thurgh thenne.

(4062-66)

When their grain is ground, John goes out to get Bayard, finds
him gone, and sets up a great outcry. The miller's wife, who has
seen the horse racing after the mares but is not an accomplice in
Symkin's actions, rushes in and exclaims:

[2] All quotations of the fabliau are taken from the A-text printed in
Bryan and Dempster, pp. 127-47. Emphasis is supplied.

> "Allas! youre hors goth to the fen
> With wilde mares, as faste as he may go.
> Unthank come on his hand that boond hym so,
> And he that bettre sholde han knyt the reyne!"
>
> (4080-3)

Berating Aleyn for failing to put the horse in the barn and in-
structing him to lay down his sword, John sets off in pursuit with
Aleyn at his heels. For hours "thise sely clerkes rennen up and
doun" in vain, but at last, when "it was verray nyght", they catch
the horse in a ditch. Then, "wery and weet, as beest is in the
reyn", the two, John leading "Bayard in his hond", return to the
mill to ask for lodging from the man who they are sure has stolen
their grain and made fools of them. John offers silver for their
meat and drink, for, as he says, "With empty hand men may na
haukes tulle" (4134); [3] and in an equally proverbial vein, he
comments upon the accommodations offered them with "I have
herd seyd, 'man sal taa of twa thynges/ Slyk as he fyndes, or
taa slyk as he brynges'." (4129-30). Preparations for the meal
are started, and then the miller does two other things which
Chaucer juxtaposes in succeeding lines:

> And boond hire hors, it sholde namoore go loos;
> And in his owene chambre hem made a bed.
>
> (4138-9)

This whole episode, which demonstrates Symkin's guile and
brings him temporary success, unfolds in a perfectly realistic
fashion. All of the details connected with the release and capture
of the horse, as well as the scraps of inserted dialogue, are neatly
fashioned to appear completely natural in the literal context of
the action. We may ask, however, why Chaucer made these
changes in plot, for it seems likely, as the following argument will
attempt to show, that the innovations of the stallion and the
clerks' wearying chase were his own alterations rather than
differences to be found in some other unrecorded analogue.

One effect of the alterations, of course, is to help establish the
dominant rivalry upon which Professor Hart has commented, but

---

[3]   This proverb also appears in the *Wife of Bath's Prologue*, 415.

this is not all. Careful examination of the passage reveals that Chaucer has deliberately chosen his details to establish an ironic parallel between this episode and the succeeding scene in which the clerks gain their revenge for Symkin's theft. The development of this parallel specifically equates the two major scenes of the tale and thus provides a structural balance which emphasizes the all-encompassing irony arising from Chaucer's total modifications of the fabliau. In the French version the only irony results from the chance that the clerks unwittingly repay the miller for his theft, but Chaucer loads the *Reeve's Tale* with details which exist primarily for their ironic impact. In the words of Germaine Dempster:

Most of what is said [in the initial portraits] is calculated to strike as strong a contrast as possible with the amusing denouement: the miller swaggers about armed with daggers and knives that he may look the more ridiculous when beaten by the clerks and receiving the decisive blow from his wife; he is jealous and foolishly proud of having married a woman of 'noble kin' brought up in nunnery that we may laugh the more at his misfortunes; his wife is 'digne as water in a dich' and his daughter is to be married 'hye in-to some worthy blood of auncestrye' in order that their surrender to the clerks may appear more ridiculous and out of keeping with former expectations; and finally, Simkin is not one of those common uninteresting thieves who would steal just for the sake of profit – he is an artist, a dilettante, one who knows all the scale from 'curteous' to 'outrageous' theft and enjoys the practice of his art a hundred times more than the possession of a few pounds of meal.[4]

In the scene of the miller's triumph sketched above, much of the irony is inherent in the situation as Chaucer presents it. As a result of the trick with the horse, the clerks are delayed until so late that they have to spend the night at the mill, and thus Symkin's cleverness brings about the circumstances which make possible his own humiliation. It is primarily through imagery and visual detail, however, that Chaucer underscores this irony and makes it more pungently humorous.

When Symkin undoes Bayard's bridle and gives the stallion freedom to pursue the wild mares as desire directs, he is un-

4   Dempster, *Dramatic Irony*, p. 28.

wittingly releasing animalistic instincts other than those of the
horse, for had he not succeeded in the theft made possible by
this one action, the two clerks would have had no call for the
revenge which they later effect. Their anger at being duped both
results essentially from this one action and parallels it, for the
desire to avenge their deception unbridles all inhibitions upon
precisely those impulses within them which they share with their
stallion. As Aleyn says:

> "Als evere moot I thryve,
> If that I may, yon wenche wil I swyve.
> Some esement has lawe yshapen us;
> For, John, ther is a lawe that says thus,
> That gif a man in a point be agreved,
> That in another he sal be releved.
> Oure corn is stoln, sothly, it is na nay,
> And we han had an il fit al this day;
> And syn I sal have neen amendement
> Agayn my los, I will have esement.
> By Goddes sale, it sal neen other bee!"
>
> (4177-87)

Nor does Chaucer leave this interpretation of the double significance of the unbridling of the stallion purely to the reader's
imagination. Almost all of the formal figures of speech which are
applied to the characters within the tale compare them to animals.[5] Indeed, even the most casual reader of the *Reeve's Tale*
could hardly fail to notice the consistency of these metaphors and

---

[5]   There are only three exceptions: the wife is "digne as water in a dich"
(3964); the daughter's eyes are "grey as glas" (3974); and John says that
he lies "as a draf-sak" in his bed (4206). Of these, only the eyes grey as
glass seems to have no implications beyond the immediate descriptive appropriateness of the simile, and this phrase was so frequently used in
medieval literature as to be a stereotyped, almost meaningless image. See:
Curry, *Ideal of Personal Beauty*, pp. 51-5. By contrast John's comparison
of himself to a sack of chaff, as he lies in bed and thinks of the revenge
which Aleyn is taking upon the miller not only describes his passivity and
feeling of worthlessness but also affords us an ironic reminder that it is
the loss of a sack of grain which has put him in this condition. Similarly,
the punning metaphor which Aleyn uses when first plotting revenge ("they
sal have the *flour* of il ending", 4174) not only suggests that the miller
shall be duly rewarded but also alludes to the theft which makes him
deserve an "il ending". This latter point has been noted by Paull F. Baum,
"Chaucer's Puns", *PMLA*, LXXI (1956), 237.

similes. The wife is correlated with a magpie (3950) and a jay (4154); John is described as a roe (4086), an ape (4202), and a swine's head (4262); both clerks return to the mill as wet as beasts in the rain (4107); Aleyn and the miller fight like two pigs in a poke (4278); the miller is compared to a peacock (3926), an ape (3935), a fly (4192), and a horse (4163-4). Thus, through imagery, Chaucer insists upon the animal nature of his characters and specifically classifies those instincts which their actions within the tale reveal.

Moreover, by the use of two similes which stand out particularly, one for its grossness, the other for its apparent internal contradiction, Chaucer sets up the parallel between the scene of Symkin's triumph and that of the clerks' revenge, and thus reinforces the ironic significance of Symkin's unbridling of the stallion. In lines 4162-4 the Miller in his drunken slumber is compared to a horse:

> This millere hath so wisely bibbed ale
> That as an hors he fnorteth in his sleep,
> Ne of his tayl bihynde he took no keep.

This vivid though indelicate image is, of course, highly effective for its immediate purpose of describing the nocturnal "melodye" to which the clerks are forced to listen; but because a horse has played so important a part in the previous scene, the simile also relates Symkin to Bayard. The connection is an ironic one, however, for just as Bayard has enjoyed his freedom only to be caught eventually in a ditch, so Symkin enjoys freedom from punishment for his theft only to be humiliated by the "swyving" of his wife, who (the astute reader will remember) is earlier described as being dignified as "water in a dich" (3964). When this proverbial comparison is used in the initial portrait of the wife, it attracts attention because it so perfectly expresses the incongruity of the parson's illegitimate daughter [6] haughtily deeming herself a lady and insisting upon being called "dame". But, surely, Chaucer also had in mind the ironic relevance for the simile which would

[6] For commentary on this point see Bennett in *Essays and Studies*, pp. 7-9.

become apparent only in the scene of the clerks' revenge. Like Bayard, Symkin, the figurative horse of the second episode, is caught because of a ditch, and if we wish to think in physiological terms, we may see in this word the same kind of coarse *double-entendre* in relation to the wife's anatomy as is evident in Chaucer's use of the word "taille" (416) in the *Shipman's Tale*.[7]

The conviction that this parallel through imagery is intentional is supported not only by Chaucer's practice in his other fabliaux but also by additional details within the first scene which function with the same kind of ironic equation to the final scene. As noted above, Chaucer juxtaposes Symkin's tying of the horse ("it sholde namoore go loos") with his making up a bed for the clerks in his "owene chambre". The irony of the placement of these two statements is devastating, for even though Bayard is tied, the duplication of his instincts in the clerks is still "loos" and will take its toll upon the wife in the very bed which Symkin here prepares. Similarly loaded with irony is John's quoting of the proverb that a guest must take (i.e. be satisfied with) one of two things, either what he finds or what he brings. Since the clerks are prevented from taking away a half-bushel of the grain they brought, they do indeed "take" what they find: namely, the wife and the daughter. John's other *sententia*, "an empty hand attracts no hawks", may also be considered ironic. The image comes from falconry, where a lure, often baited with raw meat, is used to call the bird back to the falconer's hand. What is held in the hand, in other words, keeps the hawk subdued to the will of its master. Chaucer specifically tells us only nineteen lines before this proverb that John returns to the mill leading Bayard IN HIS HAND, and as demonstrated above, it is certainly Bayard who causes the whole sequence of events which end in the utter subduing of the miller. Bayard, therefore, is the lure in both major scenes. He

---

[7]   See pp. 107-8 below. Because Chaucer uses the word "tail" with sexual implications several times – indeed, the Reeve in his prologue speaks of having a "hoor heed and a grene tayl" (3878) – it is perhaps possible that Chaucer's audience would have sensed a further ironic meaning in the simile which refers to Symkin's tail ("as an hors de fnorteth in his sleep/ Ne of his tayl behynde he took no keep"). Symkin's drunken slumber, at least, certainly causes him to pay no heed to the cuckolding.

attracts the clerks away from the mill, thus allowing Symkin a temporary mastery; but, ironically, as specified by the combination of *sententia* and literal detail, the stallion in turn becomes the lure held in the hand which provides cause for the clerks' eventual mastery over Symkin's predatoriness. Furthermore, the clerks at the end of their chase are "*wery* and weet, as beest is in the reyn" (4107), and by another ironic parallel they are, in fact, in the same condition when their revenge ends at dawn, albeit for rather different reasons!

> Aleyn wax *wery* in the dawenynge,
> For he had swonken al the longe nyght . . .
>
> (4234-5)

Thus, it is by means of imagery and visual detail that Chaucer establishes between the two major scenes of his story a parallel which doubles and redoubles the irony that is his own addition to the French fabliau. It is largely this irony, of course, as it is manifested in character, situation, action, and detail, which elevates the narrative above the level of the crude farce and allows one to enjoy repeated readings of the text. The careful ironic equating of the two major scenes not only augments the zestful humor which pervades the entire tale but also tightly unifies the whole through structural balance.

The imagery which lies outside the two major scenes functions with equal ironic relevance. At the beginning of the tale Chaucer gives three portraits which intermingle in his typical fashion the rhetorical devices of *effictio* and *notatio*. As Miss Dempster has pointed out, the substance of these portraits is designed to contrast sharply with the fate of the miller and his family, but in addition to this Chaucer establishes ironic links between even the most innocent-appearing details and later parts of the narrative.

Symkin, we are told, always goes about ferociously armed with all sorts of daggers and swords in order to protect his wife "ycomen of noble kyn", of whom he is inordinately jealous:

> Ay by his belt he baar a long panade,
> And of a swerd ful trenchant was the blade.

A joly poppere baar he in his pouche; [8]
Ther was no man, for peril, dorste hym touche.
A Sheffeld thwitel baar he in his hose.

(3929-33)

Was noon so hardy that wente by the weye
That with hire dorste rage or ones pleye,
But if he wolde be slayn of Symkyn
With panade, or with knyf, or boidekyn.
For jalous folk ben perilous evermo;
Algate they wolde hire wyves wenden so.

(3957-62)

As we know, however, all this panoply is to be of no avail against
the threat of the clerks, and Chaucer subtly underscores this
paradox by having John say at the beginning of the chase which
ends in the ditch:

"Aleyn, for Cristes peyne,
Lay doun thy swerd, and I wil myn alswa.
I is ful wight, God waat, as is a raa;
By Goddes herte, he sal nat scape us bathe!

(4084-7)

Swords will hamper the clerks' pursuit of Bayard, and in terms of
the parallel scene yet to come, the two have no need of the
weapons to attain the very thing which Symkin expects to defend
by the sword. Craft applied to a cradle will suffice. In the light of
this fact, the miller's discrediting of the clerks' wit is amusingly
ironic. Smiling at John and Aleyn's precautions for watching their
grain, he thinks to himself:

". . . 'The gretteste clerkes been noght wisest men,'
As whilom to the wolf thus spak the mare.
Of al hir art ne counte I noght a tare."

(4054-6)

Even this reference to the popular fable is ironically appropriate,
for just as the mare's kick punishes the presumptuous wolf,[9] so a
horse will here be responsible for Symkin's punishment.

[8] The "is" between "he" and "in" in line 3931 of Robinson's 1957 text
is obviously a typographical error, since it not only makes nonsense of the
line and destroys the meter but also is not found in his earlier edition.
[9] See note 4055 in *The Works of Geoffrey Chaucer*, ed. W. W. Skeat, V
(Oxford, 1894-1900), 122-3, for reference to the fable.

The two similes applied to Symkin in the original portrait also have ironic associations which reach beyond their immediate surface application. "Proud as a peacock" is an utterly commonplace image, but it is likely that Chaucer's audience would have been familiar with the pseudo-natural-history lore expounded by the extremely popular medieval bestiaries and their counterpart, the allegorized *Physiologus* (versions of which exist in Latin, French, Old English, and many other European languages), and hence would have associated things other than pride with the peacock. According to popular conception, the peacock has ugly feet which contrast sharply with the beautiful TAIL which is the source of its pride. When the bird is suddenly aroused from slumber, the *Physiologus* asserts, it cries out stridently because it dreams that it has lost its beauty. Furthermore, the bestiaries compare an imprudent man to a peacock that has lost its tail.[10] The relevance of all of this popular lore to Symkin is readily apparent, if we substitute "wife" for "tail", a word which often has sexual connotations for Chaucer (see note 7). The source of Symkin's pride is his wife, yet this pride rests on the shameful foundation of her dubious ancestry, just as Symkin's own moral character might also be considered "ugly feet". Through his imprudence he does lose the source of his pride, and he certainly awakes in the night with strident cries, fearing (and rightly so) that he has lost his "tail".

The meaning of the second simile in the portrait has been disputed,[11] but in terms of ironic associations the skull "piled as an ape" (3935) offers no difficulties. Symbolically, the ape in the Middle Ages represented lechery and hypocrisy,[12] and an extant manuscript in the Museum of Cluny depicts Avarice riding on an

---

[10] See: Evans, *Animal Symbolism*, p. 312; T. H. White, ed., *The Bestiary: A Book of Beasts* (New York, 1954), p. 149; *Physiologus*, trans. James Carlill, in *The Epic of the Beast* (London, 1924), p. 220.

[11] Both Skeat and Robinson gloss "piled" as "bald". Walter Clyde Curry, "Chaucer's Reeve and Miller", *PMLA*, XXXV (1920), 201, however, argues that the word means "having thick hair" and supports his contention by reference to the *NED*. Since at the end of the tale the wife sees a "whit thyng" and thus erroneously thinks that her husband's skull is the clerk's night cap, "bald" seems to be the best translation.

[12] Droulers, *Dictionnaire*, p. 205.

ape.[13] All three of these vices are amply evident in the miller, but more significant is Chaucer's own fondness for using the ape to mean "fool". This is John's intention when he calls himself an ape (4202), and numerous other examples might be cited.[14] Thus, the early equating of Symkin to an ape foreshadows his succeeding role, and by a neat ironic twist, the nadir of humiliation comes to him when his wife mistakenly subdues him in the final brawl with a well-placed blow upon that very "piled" skull. Moreover, by a metaphor placed halfway between the first and second mentions of the miller's "piled" skull, Chaucer links the original seemingly innocent descriptive detail with its role in the final scene. Before the household retires for the night, we are told:

> Wel hath this millere vernysshed his heed;
> Ful pale he was for dronken, and nat reed.
>
> (4149-50)

Interestingly enough, it was apparently traditional to associate a certain stage of drunkenness with the ape,[15] this fact linking the intermediate reference to the miller's head to the first description; and the pale head, here metaphorically varnished, becomes 150 lines later the "whit thyng" shining in the moonlight at which the wife directs her unfortunate but well-intentioned assault.

The portrait of the daughter is the most visual of the three, and fittingly enough most of the details emphasize her rather vulgar, concupiscible appearance: "buttokes brode, and brestes rounde and hye" (3975). For the wife, Chaucer chooses two animal similes, one appearing in the portrait, the other in the transition between the two major scenes. She is pert and proud as a "pye" (3950) and jolly as a jay (4154). Both these birds are also notorious chatterers,[16] and although the wife is given only three speeches in the tale, two of them are indeed a kind of chattering which in both cases brings about ironic results. When

[13]   Evans (note 10), pp. 162-3.
[14]   See, for example: *Miller's Tale* 3389; *Canon Yeoman's Tale* 1313; Introduction to the *Prioress' Tale* 440; General Prologue 706.
[15]   See the Manciple's Prologue, 44, and Robinson's accompanying note.
[16]   This association is still as current in the twentieth century as it was in Chaucer's day. For bestiary references, see: White (note 10), p. 138.

she reports to the clerks that Bayard is chasing the wild mares, she babbles on, cursing the hand that left the reins loose, and thus she unwittingly places upon her own husband a curse which is to be fulfilled only too soon. When she is rudely awakened at dawn by Symkin's falling upon her, she shrieks out:

"Help! hooly croys of Bromeholm . . .
In manus tuas! Lord, to thee I calle!
Awak, Symond! the feend is on me falle.
Myn herte is broken; help! I nam but deed!
Ther lyth oon upon my wombe and on myn heed.
Help, Symkyn, for the false clerkes fighte!"
(4286-91)

As a result of these mistaken exclamations, John awakes and joins in the fray from which he and Aleyn emerge victorious, and in light of what is earlier said of the wife's pride and haughtiness, we may assume that when she realizes what has happened during the night, her heart may, in fact, be broken. Furthermore, each simile which connects the wife to a chattering bird immediately precedes one and then the other of the parallel scenes of trickery and mortification, and the two unfortunate speeches which verify the aptness of the comparison play a significant part within each scene, the words in the first scene ironically foreshadowing what happens in the final one. Thus, the structural parallel in the tale achieves yet another connective link.

The bestiaries afford one further bit of animal lore which is ironically appropriate to Chaucer's similes, whether or not he so intended. The deeper a horse dips its nostrils when drinking, we are told, the greater its sexual potency.[17] Symkin, of course, is dead drunk at the point where he is compared to a horse, and as far as he is concerned, the proverbial lore is utterly false: he is oblivious to his wife. Ironically, however, Chaucer very graphically states that when the wife returns to bed and mistakes John for the miller, she is surprised by her "husband's" unusual virility: "So myrie a fit ne hadde she nat ful yoore" (4230).

We may well ask to what extent all this interweaving of ironic applications was deliberate and to what extent Chaucer expected

[17] White (note 10), p. 86.

his audience to realize the subtleties of his imagery. As far as the kinds of associations based upon the bestiaries are concerned, no absolutely definite answer can be given to either question. Since this type of animal lore was extremely popular in the Middle Ages,[18] it is likely that both Chaucer and the members of his audience would be familiar with the beliefs, but was the poet consciously attempting to bring these external associations into play? A passage in the *Nun's Priest's Tale* seems to suggest that he was indeed aware of the ironic relevance of his animal references but that he was not at all certain that his audience would apprehend anything more than the surface comparison. In this tale, just before the fox confronts the rooster, we are told that Chauntecleer "soong murier than the mermayde in the see" (3270), and the narrator goes on to cite an authority for this comparison: "For Phisiologus seith sikerly/ How that they syngen wel and myrily" (3271-2). The *Physiologus* says more than this, however, about the siren,[19] and both its literal details and allegorical interpretations are ironically apt for the confrontation which immediately follows the Nun's Priest's citation of his source. The song of the siren, we are told, incurs the danger of death, and within the tale, of course, Chauntecleer's pride in his crowing is, by an ironic inversion, about to present the same sort of peril for himself. Allegorically, according to the *Physiologus*, the siren represents on the moral level the hypocrite and on the spiritual level the devil, and again, by another ironic transference, this concept is immediately enacted by the fox, who approaches Chauntecleer asserting to be his friend and saying, "Now, certes, I were *worse than a feend*,/ If I to yow wolde

[18]   There are some forty extant manuscripts of bestiaries in England, dating from the twelfth and thirtienth centuries. See: Helen M. Franc's introduction, *The Animal Kingdom, Illustrated Catalogue of an Exhibition of Manuscript Illuminations, Book Illustrations, Drawings, Cylinder Seals and Bindings* (New York, 1940-1). Moreover, Evans (note 10), p. 54, asserts: "it is probable that the *Physiologus* in its present form is made up of fragments of several books of a similar character, which were not only used as textbooks in schools, but were intended for the edification of old and young...."

[19]   *Physiologus: A Metrical Bestiary of Twelve Chapters by Bishop Theobald*, trans. Alan Wood Rendell (London, 1928), pp. 35-7.

harm or vileynye!" (3286-7). It seems obvious that in this case Chaucer chose the simile used to describe Chauntecleer's "song" precisely because the bestiary concepts about the siren could ironically foreshadow the subsequent action and by inversion underscore the theme of pride which the tale so brilliantly develops, and that he attempted to point out the significance of his comparison by citing the source for the requisite external information. Perhaps this passage proves no more than that Chaucer was aware of the possibility of extending the significance of his comparisons to animals through the relevance of popular lore associated with them, but the relative frequency with which his animal references provide opportunity for this kind of interpretation at least suggests that he was consciously drawing upon the bestiaries for added levels of ironic appropriateness. The ironic parallels which rely upon no external information and which give the *Reeve's Tale* its structural unity, however, can hardly be accidental, and in an oral presentation the poet could emphasize by voice and gesture those words and phrases which are of special significance. Even so, it is dubious that Chaucer ever expected a listener to comprehend fully when hearing the tale for the first (or even the fifth) time. He seems to have written all his fabliaux with special zest, and he may very likely have indulged his own unique ironic sensibility merely for his own enjoyment. Whatever the case, the irony of the story does come across, whether or not the reader is aware of the artistry which has created it.

VI

THE SHIPMAN'S TALE

Much of the commentary on the *Shipman's Tale* has been devoted
to questions evoked by the incongruous opening lines in which the
"hardy", brown-hued Shipman of the General Prologue calls
himself a woman:

> The sely housbonde, algate he moot paye,
> He moot *us* clothe, and he moot *us* arraye,
> Al for his owene worshipe richely,
> In which array *we* daunce jolily.
> And if that he noght may, par aventure,
> Or ellis list no swich dispence endure,
> But thynketh it is wasted and ylost,
> Thanne moot another payen for *oure* cost,
> Or lene *us* gold, and that is perilous.
>
> (11-19)

Because the tale is violently inappropriate for the two nuns on the
pilgrimage, because the subject matter resembles the Wife of
Bath's prologue, and because Dame Alys' words are echoed in
such phrases as the desire for a husband "fressh abedde" (*ST*
177; *WBT* 1259) and the assertion of the merchant's wife that as
her husband's "dettour" she will "paye ... abedde" (*ST* 413-24;
WBP 130-2, 153), scholars generally agree that Chaucer at one
time intended the wife to be the narrator of the tale and for some
reason later transferred the fabliau to the Shipman but failed to
emend the tell-tale pronouns.[1] This confusion regarding whom
the poet originally meant to have tell the story of the unsuspecting

---

[1] For arguments against this conclusion, however, see: Frederick Tupper,
"The Bearings of the Shipman's Prologue", *JEGP*, XXXIII (1934), 352-72;
R. W. Chapman, "The *Shipman's Tale* Was Meant for the Shipman",
Modern Language Notes, LXXI (1956), 4-5.

merchant's cuckolding has led to various discussions of the ultimate function of the tale within the framework of the pilgrimage.[2] If Chaucer actually wrote the narrative for the Wife of Bath, it was intended to illustrate her cynical attitude toward marriage and her concept of the proper behavior of husbands; when the Shipman becomes the narrator, the tale serves instead as a satirical jibe at the industrious class of chapmen from whom the unscrupulous sailor has stolen "ful many a draughte of wyn" in the passage from Bordeaux to England (*G. Pro.* 396-7). Since the succeeding link clearly ascribes the tale to the Shipman, Chaucer obviously preferred the latter interpretation, but the possibility of two feasible applications reminds us of two things which are often only too easy to forget: (1) that Chaucer himself is always the narrator, and (2) that the dramatic scheme of the pilgrimage cycle is only partially operative. In fact, although the surface narrative of the *Shipman's Tale* has dramatic verisimilitude for either the Shipman or the Wife of Bath, analysis of its imagery reveals an undertone which harmonizes with neither of these lusty, worldly characters, but rather reverberates that part of Chaucer's own thinking which found one of its most moving expressions in the concluding lines of the *Troilus:*

> O yonge, fresshe folkes, he or she,
> In which that love up groweth with youre age,
> Repeyreth hom fro worldly vanyte,
> ... and thynketh al nys but a faire
> This world, that passeth soone as floures faire.
> (V, 1835-41)

We may well ask, however, if a fabliau can ultimately achieve such a statement. Although the tone and the spirit of the genre would seem to deny the possibility, such is surely the case in the *Canterbury Tales* even without the evidence which imagery provides here, for the ironic detachment which Chaucer blends with

[2] See, for example: John S. P. Tatlock, *The Development and Chronology of Chaucer's Works* (London, 1907), pp. 205-9; R. M. Lumiansky, *Of Sondry Folk* (Austin, 1955), pp. 76-7; Albert H. Silverman, "Sex and Money in Chaucer's *Shipman's Tale*", *Philological Quarterly*, XXXII (1953), 329-36; William W. Lawrence, "Chaucer's *Shipman's Tale*", *Speculum*, XXXIII (1958), 56-68.

sympathy and understanding in his presentation of the characters who tell fabliaux inevitably implies that the poet himself does not share their points of view but recognizes a standard from which their deviations may be viewed as comic. In this sense, and also in terms of the poetic justice usually evident, all of Chaucer's fabliaux are essentially moral. In the *Miller's Tale*, the *Reeve's Tale*, and the *Summoner's Tale*, for example, the principal characters who offend established Christian virtues are brought to utter mortification by the very traits upon which they pride themselves. The *Shipman's Tale*, however, is one of two fabliaux in the *Canterbury Tales* in which poetic justice does not take its toll: the deceivers escape all punishment and the deceived does not realize that he has been duped. Nonetheless, Chaucer allows his own position – or one, at least, to which he gave full philosophical, if not full emotional, allegiance – to receive oblique statement. Overtly the tale presents two clearly defined concepts. One of these is true fabliau relish for quick-witted deception which achieves its ignoble ends without exposure; the other is the merchant's deeply considered philosophy of money. It is in praise of either (or perhaps both) of these concepts that the narrator, be he Shipman or Wife, exclaims at the end of his story: "God us sende/ Taillynge ynough unto oure lyves ende" (433-4); and it is precisely within the terms of these two concepts that the tale seems to have been understood by modern commentators. It also includes, however, juxtaposed in typical Chaucerian fashion to these mundane points of view, and indirectly stated through imagery and narrative detail, the traditional Christian standard against which the two concepts may be judged. In this way – as with the *Merchant's Tale*, which also permits its characters to escape without fully realized humiliation – the tale actually contains the moral standard embedded in the imagery.

In the *Shipman's Tale* Chaucer carries on the process used in the *Reeve's Tale* whereby imagery is interwoven with specific, concrete details to produce ironic implications; but the technique here does not establish a structural parallel. Instead, it intermingles all aspects of the tale in such a way as to create a tightly knit fabric in which even the most apparently inconsequential bits are significant to the total effect. By this process Chaucer clarifies the juxtaposed points of view, and, in a manner similar to that of the *Friar's Tale*, he underscores, deepens, and elucidates an ironic parallel of character which has been set up by other means.

Four image clusters dominate the tale: references to animals, diet, trade, and sex. Through ironic associations of specific images with concrete details, a pattern is established in which all four clusters are equated [3] and reduced to one level [4] which stands in contrast to the moral ideal which is also implied by means of imagery. Of these four, the "trade" cluster is paramount, not because the tale includes a greater number of actual figurative expressions in this category, but because so much emphasis is given throughout to the bourgeois concept of materialistic success.[5]

The second line informs us that the merchant was rich, and for that reason "men helde hym wys", and from this point on the philosophy of money is developed in all directions. The merchant, we learn, keeps an excellent house, much frequented by guests who appreciate his "largesse". He appears completely generous, despite the ignominiously motivated accusation of niggardliness which his wife brings against him in her first tête-à-tête with his bosom friend, the hypocrital monk. Without hesitation, he lends the requested hundred franks to Daun John, and he accepts with mild reprimand the news that his wife has spent the repayment on "array". Yet, this is not really the generosity of a magnani-

---

[3] The way in which the "identification of sex with money informs the entire tale in a meaningful way" has been brilliantly discussed by A. H. Silverman (note 2). Although he mentions only two of the various images within the tale, and although our conclusions differ radically, I am duly endebted to his article.

[4] Although this is a subtle artistic process which operates without direct reference to theology, the result is traditional. Sex, diet and trade afford opportunities for the sins of lechery, gluttony, and avarice, which are frequently linked and which Chaucer discusses together in the *Pardoner's Tale* under the theme *Radix malorum est Cupiditas*. The association of the seven deadly sins with animals, of course, is equally traditional.

[5] Gardiner Stillwell, "Chaucer's 'Sad' Merchant", *Review of English Studies*, XX (1944), 1-18, gives an interesting account (based in part on fourteenth-century documents) of the prevalence of the "good business" practices which the merchant of the *Shipman's Tale* upholds.

mous heart but rather that of calculated business policy. From the
conversation in which his wife rebukes him for reckoning his
accounts while Daun John waits to dine, we learn that giving an
outward show of wealth is part of any wise merchant's business
activity:

> "Wyf," quod this man, "litel kanstow devyne
> The curious bisynesse that we have.
> For of us chapmen, also God me save,
> And by that lord that clepid is Seint Yve,
> Scarsly amonges twelve tweye shul thryve
> Continuelly, lastynge unto oure age.
> We may wel *make chiere and good visage,*
> And dryve forth the world as it may be,
> And kepen oure estaat in pryvetee
> Til we be deed . . .
>
> (224-33)

The rationale behind this conviction becomes apparent in his
later conversation with Daun John about the loan. If a merchant
has a reputation for success, he can borrow readily when the need
arises:

> We may creaunce whil we have a name;
> But goldlees for to be, it is no game.
>
> (289-90)

The wife assumes, or pretends to, that her own extravagant array
helps serve this ultimate purpose, and when her husband asks
about the hundred franks which the monk says has been repaid
to her, she vigorously asserts her role in this philosophy of
commercial façade:

> For by my trouthe, I have on myn array,
> *And nat on wast*, bistowed every deel;
> And for *I have bistowed it so weel*
> *For youre honour*, for Goddes sake, I seye,
> As be nat wrooth, but lat us laughe and pleye.
>
> (418-22)

The merchant seems to accept this argument and merely replies
that she should not be "so large"; prudence is also necessary if
the investment is not to exceed the possible profit. He is really
more concerned about the possibility that, should she again

neglect to tell him of business matters, he might offend a client, as he fears he has his friend:

> ". . . by God, as that I gesse
> That ye han maad a manere straungenesse
> Bitwixen me and my cosyn daun John.
> Ye sholde han warned me, er I had gon,
> That he yow hadde an hundred frankes payed
> By redy token; and heeld hym yvele apayed,
> For that I to hym spak of chevyssaunce;
> Me semed so, as by his contenaunce.
> But nathelees, by God, oure hevene kyng,
> I thoughte nat to axen hym no thyng.
> I prey thee, wyf, ne do namoore so;
> Telle me alwey, er that I fro thee go,
> If any dettour hath in myn absence
> Ypayed thee, lest thurgh thy necligence
> I myghte hym axe a thing that he hath payed."
> (385-99)

To insult one's associates would be a business policy as bad as an external display of wealth is good.

Ironically, the merchant's adherence to his philosophy provides the opportunity for his cuckolding. Before leaving on a business trip which is to involve borrowing money on his reputation, he invites Daun John to partake of the "largesse" which has helped establish that good name. In accord with the proper prudence, he must reckon the state of his finances before undertaking the venture, and while he is thus engaged with bags of money and account books behind the "pryvetee" of his "countourdore", Daun John has opportunity for an equally private reckoning with the wife, in which he agrees to give her the hundred franks and she to do him "what plesance and service" that she may. The consummation of this agreement occurs, of course, while the merchant is away. As he "gooth . . . faste and bisily/ Aboute his nede, and byeth and creaunceth" (302-3), Daun John is going equally busily (318) about HIS need, having paid for its satisfaction with borrowed money. Thus, the monk engages in his friend's own trade, with his friend's money, to purchase a merchandise which is, theoretically, his friend's exclusive marital right.

The irony inherent in the situation of the husband's money being used to buy the wife's favors appears in the two major analogues of the *Shipman's Tale*,[6] but Chaucer intensifies its impact and alters its ultimate significance by the inclusion of the money philosophy. Nor does his manipulation of the irony terminate with this paralleling of the merchant's commercial activities and Daun John's attainment of, first, opportunity and then, desired goal.

Unlike the monk, the merchant is no hypocrite. Within the limitations of his philosophy, he is a sober and upright citizen who lives honestly by the standards in which he believes. Yet, ironically, the two men – one honest, one flagrantly not so – both operate in precisely the same way. Daun John takes the initiative in establishing the close friendship with the merchant, and he always comes to the household laden with gifts to delight everyone from the master to the meanest servant. As his subsequent actions reveal, however, his generosity and friendliness are but means to his own profit, the attainment of the merchant's wife. So too, the merchant is generous and concerned with pleasing people as a means to HIS own profit, money. Thus, the "cosynage" between them, which the monk has originally asserted to ingratiate himself with the merchant, is in essence real – they are kin by action if not by blood – and the brotherhood which they have sworn becomes, therefore, doubly ironic:

> Thus been they knyt with eterne alliaunce,
> And ech of hem gan oother for t'assure
> Of bretherhede, whil that hir lyf may dure.
>
> (40-2)

Although Daun John soon breaks this "eternal alliance" by adultery, it nonetheless remains intact, for the two are unwittingly akin in method of gain. Similarly, when the monk denies his loyalty to the merchant in order to gain the wife's confidence, the ostensibly casual comparison which he uses becomes ironically relevant. He says, speaking more truthfully than usual:

---

[6] For Boccaccio's *Decameron*, VIII, 1, and Sercambi's *Novella de Avaritia et Luzuria*, see: Bryan and Dempster, pp. 439-46.

He is na moore cosyn unto me
Than is this leef that hangeth on the tree!
I clepe hym so, by Seint Denys of Fraunce,
To have the moore cause of aqueyntaunce
Of yow, which I have loved specially . . . .
(149-53)

The merchant is in fact no more related to the monk than is the hanging leaf, but all three have something in common; for, as the leaf draws its sustenance from the tree, so the monk derives his sensual satisfaction from the merchant's household, and so the merchant draws his monetary life-blood from his commercial associates. The "cosynage" [7] exists, whether avowed or denied; and yet the moral motivation of the two men seems strikingly dissimilar. But is it?

For the Shipman the moral question is surely non-existent. It is Chaucer who has given us, at some length, the details which establish the paradoxical parallel between the honest man and the thorough scoundrel, and it is he who emphasizes their equality through the pattern resulting from his technique in handling formal imagery.

The most obvious equating of trade (the merchant's goal) with fornication (the monk's goal) occurs at the end of the tale in the pun which has been noted by many commentators.[8] When the wife is giving her explanation of the receipt of Daun John's re-payment of the loan, she offers her husband precisely the bargain which she has already fulfilled with the monk:

Ye han mo slakkere dettours than am I!
For I wol paye yow wel and redily
Fro day to day, and if so be I faille,

[7] Although it is tempting to see a pun in the monk's assertion of "cosynage", the earliest documented reference to the ME "cosin" meaning "fraud" or "trickery" is dated 1453. See: Hans Kurath and Sherman M. Kuhn, *Middle-English Dictionary* (Ann Arbor, 1960), part c.5, p. 627. Of course, the OF "cosin", meaning "dupe", provides pun possibilities: when Daun John "claymeth" the merchant "as for cosynage", there is more truth in the idea that he is claiming the merchant as his dupe than as his relative.
[8] See, for example: Silverman, pp. 329-30; Claude Jones, "Chaucer's Taillynge Ynough", *Modern Language Notes*, LII (1937), 570; Robert A. Caldwell, "Chaucer's Taillyinge Ynough, Canterbury Tales, B²1624", *Modern Language Notes*, LV (1940), 262-5; Helge Kökeritz, "Rhetorical Word Play in Chaucer", *PMLA*, LXIX (1954), 952.

> I am youre wyf; score it upon my taille,
> And I shal paye as soone as ever I may.
>
> (413-17)

"Taille", meaning here both "record of account" and "pudendum", anticipates by a few lines the metaphor in which the wife asserts, "By God, I wol nat paye yow but abedde!" (424). This obvious *double-entendre* serves to clarify earlier associations of sex and trade which are sprinkled throughout the narrative, and when the merchant goes on to admonish his wife not to be "so large" in the future but to "keep bet" his "good" (431-2), we automatically include in his possessions not only his money but also his wife's body. The monk, we realize, has already made this identification during the scene of negotiation for the loan when the merchant says:

> My gold is youres, whan that it yow leste,
> And nat oonly my gold, but my *chaffare*.
> Take what yow list, God shilde that ye spare.
>
> (284-6)

The "chaffare" which the monk wants, of course, is the wife, nor does he "spare". By like token, we may be sure that although the wife is instructed to report hereafter when any "dettour" has "ypayed" her during her husband's absence (397-8), she will not do so if the payment involves both of these levels of meaning.

Earlier in the tale, when the merchant is philosophizing about his profession, first to his wife and then to the monk, he unwittingly draws the same double implications himself. Speaking of the difficulties of operating at a profit in an unstable world subjected to the vagaries of "hap and fortune", he says that he has "greet necessitee" to advise himself "upon this queynte world" (235-6); and, did he but realize, it is not so much the curious world which stands in need of investigation at this point as it is his wife's commercial attitude toward her "queynte", a word Chaucer favors for female anatomy.[9] To the monk the merchant asserts:

---

[9] Chaucer uses "queynte" for female anatomy in several tales: *Miller's T.* 3276; *W. of B. Pro.* 332, 444. The adjectival form of the word appears in the *Merchant's Tale*, 2061, with perhaps the same *double-entendre* as found here.

> But o thyng is, ye knowe it wel ynogh,
> Of chapmen, that hir moneie is hir plogh.
>
>   (287-8)

For obvious reasons, the plow is a common phallic symbol.[10] Although the merchant certainly does not means his statement to give any such implications, the sexual possibilities of his metaphor have an ironic appropriateness of which he remains completely unaware. The wife complains, perhaps truthfully, to the monk about her husband's neglect of intimate attentions. The concern for making money apparently occupies all his energies, and the virility which he displays in the final scene is a result, we are told, of his release from financial worries:

> And al that nyght in murthe they bisette;
> For he was riche and cleerly out of dette.
>
>   (375-6)

Thus, money has been his sexual "plow" not only in the sense that for its sake he has failed to satisfy his wife, but also in that a hundred franks of his own money have, so to speak, provided a sharecropper to tend to the neglected tilling!

Several of the images in the "trade" cluster relate to both sexual activity and the "animal" group of references, and thus the range of equated associations widens to include animalistic impulses. When talking to the monk in the first scene, for example, the wife assesses the value of her husband with a comparison

---

[10]   Two literary instances in which the image is used in this way come to mind. In the final lines of the thirteenth-century Middle-English fabliau *Dame Siriz* (ed. Thomas Wright, *Anecdote Literaria* (London, 1841), p. 13), the witch says to the clerk for whom she has been pandering:

> And loke that thou hire *tille*
>   And strek out hire thes,
> God ʒeve the muchel kare
> ʒeif that thou hire spare.

In Book IV of *De Rerum Natura* Lucretius writes:

> denique cum membris collatis flore fruuntur
> aetatis, iam cum praesagit gaudia corpus
> atque in eost Venus ut *muliebria conserat arva*,
> adfigunt avide corpus . . .
>
>   (1105-8)

I do not intend, of course, to imply that Chaucer knew either of these works but merely to point out that the phallic association is widespread.

which appears so often in the *Canterbury Tales* as to be almost a cliché: "he is noght worth at al/ In no degree the value of a flye" (170-1).[11] This commonplace expression, however, gains a particularly ludicrous effect in this instance since it is her husband's virility which she is evaluating. To describe the same sexual activity, the monk says in reply to the wife's question about his early rising:

> "Nece ... it oghte ynough suffise
> Fyve houres for to slepe upon a nyght,
> But it were for an old appalled wight,
> As been thise wedded men, that lye and dare
> As in a fourme sit a wery hare,
> Were al forstraught with houndes grete and smale.
>
> (100-5)

After this comment which incorporates the animal traditionally symbolic of lechery,[12] the monk blushes, perhaps because the image of the hare crouching in its lair evokes a more graphic picture of his lascivious thoughts [13] than of the weariness which is the overt topic of his banter. This image is linked to trade later on in the tale by a possible pun on the word "form", which in Chaucer's day meant "bench" as well as "an animal's burrow".[14] The monk, in reporting that he has repaid the loan, says with a neat touch of implied blackmail:

---

[11]   See also: *Reeve's T.* 4192; *Frank T.* 1132; *Canon Y.'s T.* 1150; *Parl. of F.* 501. Dean S. Fansler, *Chaucer and the Roman de la Rose* (New York, 1914), pp. 74-7, discusses the popularity of this method of "picturesque negation" and asserts that Chaucer and Jean de Meun use it more frequently than other medieval writers.

[12]   See pp. 83-4 above.

[13]   The same image appears in the *Early English Metrical Lives of the Saints* to describe the position of a foetus:

> Al round hit lyth in the wombe, i-buyd as an hare
> Whan he in forme lyth, for hit is somdel nare,
> Al i-buyd the legges, his nolde noʒt elles vie,
> The heles atte buttokes, the kneon in aither eye,
> The heved i-boued a-doun-ward ...

(See: Thomas Wright, ed., *Popular Treatises on Science Written during the Middle Ages* (London, 1841), p. 139.) This passage would seem to confirm the interpretation that Daun John's simile is pornographic.

[14]   According to the *NED* (s.v. "form"), John of Trevisa uses "forme" to mean "bench" in his translation of the *Polychronicon* (1387).

> But nathelees, I took unto *oure* dame,
> Youre wyf, at hom, the same gold ageyn
> *Upon youre bench*; she woot it wel, certeyn,
> By certeyn tokenes that I kan hire telle.
>
> (356-9)

That he intends the word "bench" to be a metaphor with anatomical implications is suggested not only by the fact that this detail would be otherwise pointless but also by his fondness for this sort of sly insinuation. When he asks to borrow the money, he gives a false reason which is nonetheless ironically the truth and which contains a nasty hypocritical barb (274):

> O thyng, er that ye goon, if it may be,
> I wolde prey yow; for to lene me
> An hundred frankes, for a wyke or tweye,
> For *certein beestes* that I moste beye,
> To stoore with a place that is oures.
> God helpe me so, *I wolde it were youres!*
> I shal nat faille surely of my day,
> Nat for a thousand frankes, a mile way.
> But lat this thyng be secree, I yow preye,
> For yet to-nyght thise beestes moot I beye.
>
> (269-78)

In this passage he deliberately connects trade with animals, which in turn are equated with fornication through his real reason for wanting the money.

Daun John's innuendo is also responsible for the parallel position of the fourth image cluster, diet. When bidding farewell to the merchant, he advises his friend to govern his diet "Atemprely, and namely in this hete", and he concludes this unctuous bit of advice with the ambiguous statement, "Bitwix us two nedeth no strange fare" (261-3). Although this is overtly a statement of their close friendship, the monk's choice of language gives covert metaphorical expression to his own intemperate appetite for the merchant's wife. In the vocabulary of courtly love, "strange", of course, is a customary term for the woman's disdain of the lover,[15] and the monk, secure in his bargain with the wife, can indeed thus imply that his advances, his consumption of "fare", will

[15] Chaucer uses "straunge" in this way elsewhere: *Parl. of Fowls* 584; *R. of R.* 2312.

meet with no more rejection than do the husband's. Because of
the figurative meaning given to food in this passage, the various
literal references to dining which occur some fifty lines earlier
tend to partake of the same ironic metaphorical interpretation. As
soon as Daun John's bargain with the wife is arranged, we are
told:

> And with that word he caughte hire by the flankes,
> And hire embraceth harde, and kiste hire ofte.
> "Gooth now youre wey," quod he, "al stille and softe,
> And lat us dyne as soone as that ye may;
>
> (202-5)

If he did not go on to add a comment about the time of day,
even the wife might well assume that "dyne" referred to their
agreement; but as it is, she rushes up to the counting house, be-
rates her husband for "fasting" while he casts his sums, and asks
if he is not ashamed to keep Daun John from dining. The unwitting appropriateness of this bit of dialogue to the sexual situation is self-evident – "Of chapmen . . . moneie is hir plogh".

Amusingly enough, after the cuckolding the merchant repeats
the key word from the monk's diet metaphor when he complains
to his wife, "ye han maad a manere straungenesse/ Bitwixen me
and my cosyn Daun John" (386-7). The lack of "strange fare"
which the two men share on the sexual level results in a "straunge-
nesse" on another level, a restraint in their friendship which even
the unsuspecting husband senses, although he characteristically
accredits it to money matters, to his ignorance of the repayment
of the loan with which Daun John has supposedly purchased
"certein beestes", beasts which are in reality the "fare" not
"strange". Tortuous as the syntax of the preceding statement may
be, its circularity nonetheless demonstrates what Chaucer has
done with the four image clusters in this tale. By such interrelating of reference, he erases all apparent levels of distinction
so that trade, sex, and appetite are reduced to mere animalism.

One final group of images completes this pattern. Four times
within the tale when Chaucer wishes to describe joy which his
characters feel, he chooses to compare their emotions to the
apparent lightheartedness of birds. The first of these similes

appears early in the narrative when we are told that the merchant is so pleased to have Daun John claim "cosynage" with him that he never once denies that the relationship is true:

> The monk hym claymeth as for cosynage;
> And he agayn, he seith nat ones nay,
> But was *as glad therof as fowel of day*;
> For to his herte it was a greet plesaunce.
> Thus been they knyt with eterne alliaunce,
> And ech of hem gan oother for t'assure
> Of bretherhede, while that hir lyf may dure.
> (36-42)

Only fourteen lines later the same image is used to express the delight which the merchant's servants have in Daun John's visits:

> He noght forgat to yeve the leeste page
> In al that hous; but after hir degree
> He yaf the lord, and sitthe al his meynee,
> Whan that he cam, som manere honest thyng;
> For which they were as glad of his comyng
> *As fowel is fayn whan that the sonne up riseth.*
> (46-51)

Because the monk dispenses gifts with a liberal hand, he is eagerly welcomed. Later on, when the wife's financial worries have been mitigated by the arrangement just made with Daun John, she departs from his company "as jolif as a pye" (209); and still later, when the merchant has successfully completed his business negotiations in Paris, he goes home as "murie as a papejay" (369).

In three of these comparisons, the joy described results directly from materialistic profit: gifts for the servants, a hundred franks for the wife, a thousand franks for the husband. Thus, the animal cluster of images is further tied to the trade theme, and by the mention of one concrete detail it is also linked to the diet cluster. One gift which Daun John always brings to the merchant's house, we are told, is fowl for the dinner table ("And volatyl, as ay was his usage", 72). Because his generosity is a covert device to give him easy access to the merchant's house and ultimately to the merchant's wife, this gift is also related to the sex theme. In this group of associations, then, as in the others previously discussed,

Daun John is the catalyst through which the four image clusters are reduced to one essence.

But what purpose controls this ironic equating of images? What does the technique do to the tale as a whole? In terms of structure, of course, the interrelating of image and literal details tightens the unity of the narrative, but the major result is apparent in terms of ultimate meaning. As previously demonstrated, Chaucer has manipulated various elements of the tale so as to establish an ironic parallel between the honest merchant and the hypocritical monk. The full significance of this parallel, however, is not clear without the similar ironic paralleling of the four image clusters. Because of their interweaving associations, sex, diet, animalism, and trade become as one: they are equated on a single horizontal plane. Thus, Chaucer embodies within the tale a value judgment on the mercantile philosophy which is overtly extolled. If trade, like sex and diet, is merely animal in nature, then it is not a preoccupation worthy of man's proper state, for man stands higher on the scale of being than the animal partly because of his spiritual potentialities, his ability to apprehend the eternal which does not pass "soone as floures faire". The merchant, however, is so immersed in his doctrine of profit and loss that he functions only in terms of "worldly vanytee"; he fails, in other words, to make use of the major attribute which elevates man above the animal. Despite all his virtues, he deserves to be cheated as he is because his moral philosophy rests upon the wrong foundation.

In this light, Chaucer's comparisons of the merchant to a parrot and the wife to a magpie have further significance. Both these birds can be taught to speak; yet, however human this ability may make them seem, they remain animals and nothing more. The merchant and his wife are fittingly so described, for although they are ostensibly human beings, their concerns (as the equating of images establishes) are merely animal in nature. As stated before, this point of view is Chaucer's; it is obviously not appropriate for the narrator, be he Shipman or Wife of Bath; nor does the merchant in the tale have any awareness of the concept. Yet, it is only when the flaw in the merchant's whole view of life is recognized that the successful deception of the honest, generous, warm-hearted man becomes acceptably just.[16] The parrot, to which the merchant is compared, has a skull so thick, say the bestiaries, "that if it has to be taught anything, it needs to be admonished with blows. Although it really does try to copy what its teacher is saying, it wants an occasional crack with an iron bar." [17] Like the parrot's syllables, the merchant's virtues are unsatisfactory imitations, and Chaucer's story in which the apparently moral man is punished may be intended as just such a blow, not for the character in the tale but for the poet's fourteenth-century contemporaries.

The contrasting point of view juxtaposed to the mercantile philosophy is made more explicit that this, however, for just as Chaucer indirectly asserts that the world of trade and the virtues engendered by the merchant's philosophy are not worthy of man's true estate, so he also implies the positive standard from which his characters deviate; and, he sets forth the latter, as he does the former, by an ironic use of imagery and specific detail. Indeed, the first simile, which appears in line 9, together with its surrounding context actually contains the essence of the whole narrative. Introducing the wife, the narrator says:

> And compaignable and revelous was she,
> Which is a thyng that causeth more *dispence*
> Than *worth* is al the chiere and reverence
> That men hem doon at festes and at daunces.
> Swiche salutaciouns and contenaunces
> *Passen as dooth a shadwe upon the wal;*
>
> (4-9)

Here, in what is essentially a rhetorical *digressio* placed in one of the two positions (beginning and ending) most recommended by rhetoricians for emphasis, we have the germ of the mercantile philosophy (in the words "dispence" and "worth") and also an oblique statement of its futility: what is attained by expenditure

---

[16] The explanation offered by Lumiansky (note 2), p. 75, does not seem an adequate justification for the successful duping of the merchant. The fact that his absorption in business makes him "boring" to his unworthy wife is hardly satisfactory reason for allowing her sensuality to triumph over his moral superiority, although in dramatic terms with the Shipman as narrator it may seem quite sufficient to him.

[17] White, p. 113.

of money is fleeting and insubstantial. Although these first lines attach the concept only to the social compliments of men, they imply that the desired goal of "dispence" is the attainment of something which will not "passen as dooth a shadwe upon the wal"; yet, the use of this Biblical image [18] simultaneously reminds the audience, perhaps more surely in the Catholic fourteenth century than in the partially agnostic twentieth, that only the Kingdom of God, which no "dispence" can purchase, is eternal.[19] Thus, indirectly, Chaucer introduces both the paradox which renders all monetary endeavors vain and the spiritual alternative: to attain something which will not pass as a shadow, man must concern himself with his spiritual home, with the "endelees blisse of hevene" (Parson's T., 1075). This, and only this, must be man's major preoccupation if he is to achieve the everlastingness which his human nature allows him to apprehend and desire – if, in other words, he is to justify his elevation above the animal. Chaucer ironically allows the narrator of the tale to reveal this Christian concept unwittingly by applying it to trivial social behavior, and through a similar use of irony the poet keeps the idea visible throughout the ensuing story.

References to God and to the religious observances by which man maintains touch with the divine appear again and again in the narrative, but always in connection with completely irreverent actions. Chaucer has the cuckolding, for example, occur on a Sunday. Thus, the man who has vowed his life to the service of God and the woman who constantly calls upon God to witness her veracity celebrate the Sabbath with a deed which climaxes all of

[18] Chaucer uses the image in the Parson's Tale, 1069, to express the transitoriness of worldly riches as opposed to the "endeless blisse of hevene" and ironically in the Merchant's Tale, 1315, to contrast the impermanence of material possessions with the steadfastness of a wife; the fleeting shadow also appears in Job, XIV, 2, to describe the brevity of man's earthly life:

Home ... Qui quasi flos egreditur et conteritur,
Et fugit velut umbra, et nunquam in eodem statu permanet.

[19] Perhaps one of the most effective medieval expressions of the transitoriness of worldly wealth and fame in contrast to the transcendent glory and permanence of Heaven, which can be won only by accepting the love of Christ, is the thirteenth-century lyric, "A Luue-Ron", by the Franciscan friar, Thomas de Hales.

their unholy actions.[20] Furthermore, they perpetrate this deception with oaths sworn in the name of God. Although many of Chaucer's characters are notorious swearers, the three protagonists in this tale are unusually fond of supporting every assertion from sincere truth to blatant lie with religious oaths. Within 234 lines of dialogue, twenty-six statements invoke the testimony of God; nine others call upon Christ, the Virgin Mary, and various saints for verification; and Daun John swears by his breviary, his profession, his truth, and heaven's bliss. God is called to witness that Daun John wishes the place for which he is going to buy "certein beestes" belonged to the merchant, or that the wife thought the monk gave her the hundred franks as an expression of gratitude for her husband's friendship. Although supporting such falsehoods with divine authority is completely irreverent, the characters involved never once seem aware of the fact. Here, as elsewhere in the tale, the FORMS of religion are maintained without any sense of their meaning. Mass is said in the merchant's household, but Chaucer shows the meaninglessness of the ceremony in this setting by juxtaposing it to one of his four image clusters. The wife concludes the speech in which she abuses the merchant for reckoning his accounts with "What! lat us heere a messe, and go we dyne" (223), and a few lines later we are told:

> And doun he gooth, no lenger wolde he lette.
> But *hastily* a messe was ther seyd,
> And *spedily* the tables were yleyd,
> And *to the dyner faste they hem spedde,*
> And richely this monk the chapman fedde.
>
> (250-4)

Equally ironic and equally meaningless are the oaths which the wife and Daun John swear to each other. The monk asserts:

> For on my porthors here I make an ooth
> That nevere in my lyf, for lief ne looth,
> Ne shal I of no conseil yow biwreye."
>
> (131-3)

[20] Chaucer does something very similar in the *Troilus* when he has Criseyde betray her Trojan lover upon the very day which she has vowed will end her temporary separation from him.

Yet, the pledge on the breviary means nothing to him, for he later tells the merchant that he has given the money to the wife and leaves her in the difficult position of providing an adequate explanation. He also swears by his profession that he has claimed "cosynage" with the merchant only in order to have access to the wife, whom he says, he has loved "specially aboven alle wommen" (149-55); yet, his profession requires a vow of chastity. The wife, in turn, vows that she will never betray the confidence of the monk even though she should go to hell:

> By God and by this porthors I yow swere,
> Though men me wolde al into pieces tere,
> Ne shal I nevere, for to goon to helle,
> Biwreye a word of thyng that ye me telle . . .
>
> (135-8)

Although she speaks here of the possibility of damnation, her behavior throughout shows that "helle" is nothing more than a word to her.[21]

Nothing within the tale indicates that this empty use of religious forms and terminology results from cynicism; the characters seem, instead, to suffer from a spiritual blindness or obtuseness which allows them to utilize the material symbols of spiritual existence for purely earthly purposes without realizing the incongruity. They mechanically adhere to the externals of religious practice without the least understanding of or concern for the inner significance. Ironically, this obtuseness at times leads them unwittingly to the truth which underlies the tale. The wife, for example, when berating her husband for counting his money and delaying the meal, inadvertently evaluates the mercantile philosophy aright: "The devel have part on alle swiche rekenynges!" (218).

By this indirect and ironic method, then, Chaucer keeps the

---

[21] The observance of religious form without belief is naively illustrated by the tale of "The Wicche, the Bagge and the Bisshop" in Robert Mannyng's *Handlyng Synne*. Since this handbook, based upon the French *Manuel de Pechiez* and written during the first decade of the 1300s, was designed to popularize moral theology, it seems likely that the practice which Chaucer illustrates in the *Shipman's Tale* was a question of real concern to the fourteenth century.

spiritual ideal in the minds of his audience as a counterbalance to
the philosophy of money. It is in his handling of the merchant,
however, that the true profundity of his moral insight becomes
apparent. Both the monk and the wife are purely sensual crea-
tures, and their deviations from all moral standards are plainly
obvious; yet, they succeed in cheating the merchant who is overtly their moral superior. Since this superiority is based upon a
worldly code of values, however, it comes no closer to the spiritual
fountainhead of true virtue than does their vacuous use of religious formulae. That it does not is both ironic and pathetic, for
the merchant does possess spiritual longings, and to this extent
he demonstrates impulses worthy of man's elevation above the
animal. He is vividly aware of the transitory nature of earthly
things, as his reference to the dread which chapmen must have of
"hap and fortune" shows. Because riches are so fleeting, he says
of himself and merchants in general:

> We may wel make chiere and good visage,
> And dryve forth the world as it may be,
> And kepen oure estaat in pryvetee,
> Til we be deed, or elles that we pleye
> A pilgrymage, or goon out of the weye.
>
> (230-4)

Despite his longing for something eternal, he is as blind as his
wife and the monk to spiritual reality. He hopes to solve the
problem by increasingly careful manipulation of the tokens of
worldly exchange, not realizing the futility of such an endeavor.
Ironically, he mentions at this very point a possible path to the
everlastingness which he desires, but he does not see it in its true
light. A pilgrimage for him is either a vacation from serious business, a time for "pleye", or a convenient excuse for escaping from
unmanageable financial difficulties.

It is because he is so conscious of the instability of human
fortune that the "cosynage" offered by the monk gives his heart
such "greet plesaunce". To be "knyt with *eterne* alliaunce" (40)
to a friend affords great joy to the man who longs for something
eternal but can envision achieving it only by clever barter. In this
"bretherhede" there is apparently no buying and selling, only

mutual love, and with pathetic eagerness the merchant grasps at this fulfillment of his spiritual need. As subsequent events show, of course, he has gone as far astray in this solution as he does in his mercantile philosophy. Chaucer underscores the pathos of the merchant's joy by the simile which he uses to describe the emotion ("as glad therof as fowel of day"). When he repeats this image immediately afterwards to express the pleasure the servants have in Daun John's liberality, he indirectly reveals the ironic relationship of the two episodes. The servants' joy results from materialistic profit, the merchant's from the absence of materialistic considerations; but, the merchant is wrong in his evaluation of the situation, for the concept of profit is there, hypocritically concealed in the monk's heart. Ironically, the merchant, who has founded his whole life upon the doctrine of profit and loss, is deceived by what is merely a baser version of his own tactics, and he accepts as true friendship what is really a business venture for Daun John. When the wife, however, makes her final excuses to the husband, she unwittingly evaluates the friendship correctly:

> He took me certeyn gold, that woot I weel . . .
> For, God it woot, I wende, withouten doute,
> That he hadde yeve it me bycause of yow,
> To doon therwith myn honour and my prow,
> For cosynage, and *eek for beele cheere*
> *That he hath had ful ofte tymes heere.*
>
> (404-10)

The monk was paying for the hospitality of friendship. Even though her assertion is a deliberate lie, she comes closer to the truth than her husband ever has. The merchant's curious vision, which enables him to see a spiritual goal but leaves him blind to the one means of attaining that goal, allows him to accept illusion for reality.

Thus, Chaucer's technique of an ironic interweaving of image and concrete detail transforms an overt fabliau into a moral exemplum. The moral, however, is not a simple one. Although the merchant's philosophy might easily be related to greed (and any good medieval man would readily assent that avarice is a deadly sin),[22] Chaucer deliberately denies this motive to his character and depicts him instead as a generous man of seeming virtue. Yet, this man of noble instincts, who conforms superficially to the external patterns of traditional virtue, has made one disastrous and pathetic mistake which negates all of his positive qualities. He has blindly and unknowingly accepted a worldly standard of values in place of spiritual truth; and, as everything in the tale, denouement included, shows, he is therefore doomed. Thus exposed, the merchant stands as an object lesson to Chaucer's contemporaries of a danger not easily perceived. When the mercantile philosophy directs men's lives, they are fallible, however well-intentioned and virtuous their behavior may be. They sin without knowing that they do, and this is the most dangerous of all moral quandaries.[23]

The concluding couplet of the tale rounds out the irony of the whole:

> Thus endeth now my tale, and God us sende
> Taillynge ynough unto oure lyves ende. Amen.
>
> (433-4)

[22] Morton W. Bloomfield, *The Seven Deadly Sins* (Ann Arbor, 1952), p. 74, notes that with the increased importance of merchants and the bourgeoisie in the later Middle Ages, "avarice gained increasing emphasis as the cause of all sin, but it did not replace pride officially" (see also p. 95). Biblical authority for this view of avarice was supplied by *I Timothy*, vi, 10, the *radix malorum est cupiditas* which Chaucer's Pardoner uses as his constant theme.

The wide-spread, popular knowledge of the seven sins resulted from a decree of the Lateran Council that the priest should instruct the people in this doctrine, among others. Vast varieties of instructional materials were subsequently produced which were largely responsible for the transference of the concept from theologians to the people and from Latin to the vernacular (*ibid.*, pp. 91-2). Preachers and confessors "impressed the cardinal sins so deeply on the popular mind that the Sins came to occupy a much more important place in the lay conception of religion than their position in theology warranted" (p. 93).

[23] Theologically, of course, this position is dubious, but within this tale theology merely forms an implicit backdrop against which human reality exposes its inadequacies. From a purely human point of view, the merchant's moral dilemma is not only possible but also commonplace, as the growth of bourgeois attitudes in Chaucer's day and the chorus of protests against them evidenced only too well. See Johan Huizinga, *The Waning of the Middle Ages* (London, 1924), p. 19.

When the narrator concludes on this note, it is obvious that, although he has ostensibly been responsible for every word in the story, he does not understand the moral any more than do the characters whose actions he has described. Whether we are to think of "taillynge" here as meaning what the wife intends in her use of the word seventeen lines before or as a reckoning of money,[24] the narrative has just demonstrated that both of these are the last things which man should request from God. With this ironic verification of the difficulty of the moral problem, Chaucer ends his *Shipman's Tale*, a fabliau which sets forth a penetrating moral insight by ironic juxtaposition of sacred and mundane themes yet sacrifices none of the zest and humor of the genre to which it outwardly belongs.

[24] Caldwell (note 8) argues that the narrator's "taillynge" is not intended as a pun meaning "sexual intercourse", but should be understood literally as "business dealings". Because of the nature of the business dealings in the tale, however, one fails to see how the double meaning can be avoided.

VII

THE MERCHANT'S TALE

Unlike most of Chaucer's fabliaux the *Merchant's Tale*, or a portion thereof, has a direct source. The essential outlines of its plot come as usual from popular tradition, the "fruit tree" story of wifely deception being found in numerous analogues all over western Europe in the late Middle Ages;[1] however, as John Livingston Lowes was the first to perceive,[2] the leisurely introduction of old January, his determination to marry, and his discussion of the pros and cons of marriage with his two "brothers", Placebo and Justinus, is a brilliant adaptation of the form, the content, and occasionally the phrasing of Eustache Deschamps' interminable *Miroir de Mariage* (c. 1381-9). In the French allegory, Franc Vouloir, a man no longer young ("Ton eage est encor ou moyen"[3]), is urged by his counsellors, Folie, Desir, Servitute, and Faintise, to take a wife. After hearing their various eulogies of the wedded state, Franc Vouloir recalls that things he has heard from husbands do not precisely coincide with the statements of his four "treschers amis", and he decides to ask for further advice from another friend, Repertoire de Science. The latter replies with a lengthy letter containing all the anti-feminist doctrine dear to medieval taste and urging his friend to select a spiritual marriage rather than an earthly. Franc Vouloir weighs

[1] Germaine Dempster, "The 'Merchant's Tale'", *Modern Philology*, XXXIV (1936), 133-54; Bryan and Dempster, pp. 333-56.

[2] John Livingston Lowes, "Chaucer and the *Miroir de Mariage*", *Modern Philology*, VIII (1910), 165-86.

[3] *Œuvres Complètes d'Eustache Deschamps*, ed. Gaston Raynaud, Société des Anciens Textes Français, IX (1894), l. 89. Subsequent quotations from the *Miroir de Mariage* are taken from this edition. Emphasis is supplied.

both sides and decides in favor of the spiritual, thus illustrating the poet's allegorical message that by free will man may attain salvation if he rejects the world of the flesh. As Lowes and others have pointed out,[4] Chaucer has condensed and reversed this situation and yet has retained much of the subject matter and something of the *débat* form of the original. January himself, seconded by the servile Placebo, initiates the plan for taking a wife and presents the arguments in favor of marriage which Deschamps puts into the mouths of Franc Vouloir's four counsellors. Justinus, like Repertoire de Science, provides opposition to the plan, although he does not reject the idea of earthly marriage in favor of spiritual but merely urges a sensible and careful choice of a wife.[5]

For present purposes, the identification of this source is valuable in a way which the previously mentioned scholars have not considered, for several of the passages which Chaucer adapts rather literally from the French contain images which he transfers to his own text. Specifically, these passages are as follows:

> Il me semble selon leurs (i.e. husbands') diz
> Ce (i.e. marriage) n'est repos ne *paradis,*
> Mais droiz *enfers* . . .
>
> (815-17)

> Ainsi quatre de moy se partent
> Qui de griefs pensers me repartent
> De moi bouter en servitute,
> Qui par le droit de l'institute
> Et du droit du ciel premerain
> Suis plus frans que *l'oisel* du raim
> Qui peut ou il lui plaist voler . . .
>
> (523-29)

> Et si voions neis qui li *arbre*
> Sur les caillos et sur le marbre
> Croissent et font leurs *fruiz* divers,
> Ne n'yert ja nulz si granz yvers
> Que leur racine ne s'extende

[4]   Lowes (note 2); John C. McGalliard, "Chaucer's *Merchant's Tale* and Deschamps' *Miroir de Mariage*", *Philological Quarterly*, XXV (1946), 193-220; Carleton Brown, "The Evolution of the Canterbury 'Marriage Group' ", *PMLA*, XLVIII (1933), 1041-59.
[5]   McGalliard (note 4), p. 219.

En terre, et autre arbre ne rende.
Quant aux vieulx leur humeur perie,
Au jeune est forme reperie.
Ainsi se vont renouvellent ...

(117-25)

Despite the fact that Chaucer borrows these figurative references directly, paradise, the bird, the tree, and the fruit (as will be demonstrated) become integral parts of the complex ironic pattern of imagery which underlies the *Merchant's Tale* and which functions in a manner similar to that of the *Shipman's Tale* to provide a sort of moral ballast. With Chaucer the images extend their significance beyond the direct point of reference; with Deschamps they are relevant only in the immediate context. One might argue, of course, that the comparison of marriage to paradise in line 816 has certain ramifications, for as the poem develops, the attainment of spiritual paradise becomes the major issue. Indeed, in section LXI Repertoire de Science addresses Franc Vouloir thus:

Beaux filz, vueilliez y prandre garde,
Pour Dieu de marier te garde.
Laisses ces noces temporeles;
Venons aux espiritueles
Dont les embracemens sont doulz;
Faisons de *paradis* espoux ...

(6783-8)

In succeeding sections Deschamps develops the metaphor of spiritual marriage at great length, and it is within these same figurative terms that Franc Vouloir makes his final decision. The rather light introduction of the paradise image in connection with earthly marriage might, therefore, be considered a thematic foreshadowing, were it not for the fact that the original statement occurs almost six thousand lines before the reapplied metaphor appears again. No doubt Deschamps, anticipating the moral ending of his allegory, selected the phrase deliberately when introducing his protagonist's doubts of the advice from the four counsellors, but surely no reader can be expected to remember the relevant phrase over such a lengthy interval. Even if the poet did have some notion of an extended importance for his original use of the metaphor, his own prolixity destroys the possible effect. At any rate, whatever the truth may be in this instance, examination of the functioning of all the above-mentioned images in the *Miroir de Mariage* indicates that Chaucer did not borrow his intricate ironic technique in the handling of imagery from the source which provided him with these few actual figurative comparisons.[6]

To extoll the consummate artistry with which Chaucer has blended materials from his two major sources, Deschamps' marriage *débat* and the popular "fruit-tree" fabliau, so as to create an exquisitely unified whole would be merely to repeat what most twentieth-century critics have already said about the *Merchant's Tale*,[7] despite its two rather awkward cruxes.[8] Since no one has been interested primarily in Chaucer's imagery, however, this aspect of the tale has not been fully discussed, even though it is

[6] The *Miroir de Mariage* is not, of course, the only work which influenced the first part of the *Merchant's Tale*. Some seventy years ago Emil Koeppel pointed out that Chaucer had relied in part upon his own *Tale of Melibee*, which is a translation of a French condensation of the *Liber Consolationis et Consilii* of Albertanus Brixiensis, and upon another work of Albertanus, the *Liber de Amore* ("Chaucer und Albertanus Brixiensis", *Archiv*, LXXXVI (1891), 29-46). Robinson's notes also indicate various other sources or parallels, including the *Parson's Tale* and the two favorite anti-feminist tracts of the Middle Ages, St. Jerome's *Epistola Adversus Jovinianum* and Theophrastus' *Liber Aureolus de Nuptiis*, as preserved by St. Jerome. In her doctoral dissertation, *The Patristic Influence on Chaucer* (Catholic University, 1953), pp. 54-75, Sister Mary Raynelda Makarewicz points out passages from Clement of Alexandria, St. John Chrysostom, St. Jerome, and St. Augustine which parallel many of the ideas about marriage ironically incorporated into the first section of the *Merchant's Tale*; none of these statements of the Fathers, however, provided specific imagery for Chaucer.
[7] For a dissenting opinion, however, see: Robert M. Jordan, "The Non-dramatic Disunity of the *Merchant's Tale*", *PMLA*, LXXVIII (1963), 293-9.
[8] One passage difficult to explain in terms of the unity of the tale is Justinus' reference to the Wife of Bath (1685). For discussions of this problem see Robinson's note, p. 715. The long passage in praise of marriage (1267-1392) has also occasioned disagreement, largely in terms of what tone Chaucer intended to convey. See Robinson's note, p. 713; John C. McGalliard, "Chaucerian Comedy: The *Merchant's Tale*, Jonson, and Molière", *Philological Quarterly*, XXV (1946), 351-3; Albert C. Baugh, "The Merchant's Tale", *Modern Philology*, XXXV (1937), 15-26.

partially through imagery that the two portions of the story are unified. Once again, as in the *Reeve's Tale*, Chaucer here utilizes his technique of introducing figurative concepts which function in an ironic relationship to literal details of the plot, but he reverses the general structural pattern of the process as used in the *Reeve's Tale*: there, imagery in the second half of the tale ironically reproduces actual events of the first major scene; here, figurative comparisons set up in the first section ironically foreshadow the literal action of the final scene.

A number of these instances have, of course, been noted by previous commentators interested in the general artistry of the tale. In her excellent study of dramatic irony in Chaucer's works, Germaine Dempster has pointed out, in a footnote, the existence of "several veiled allusions to the events in the second half of the tale", and she mentions, among other things, that the Merchant's quoting of the proverb, "For love is blynd alday, and may nat see" (1598), "immediately connects in our minds January's first form of blindness with another form that awaits him, a tragically ironical coincidence".[9] She also calls attention to the fact that January's early statement about a husband's being able to guide a young wife "Right as men may *warm wex* with handes plye" (1430) receives ironic negation when May, determined to arrange a meeting with Damyan, makes a duplicate key to the garden by taking an impression of the original in "warm wex" (2117);[10] and in another footnote she remarks that "the relative frequency of the mentions of trees in the early part of the tale suggests intentional dramatic irony",[11] since the reader already familiar with the story cannot help thinking of the importance of a tree in the events yet to come. J. S. P. Tatlock, indirectly supporting Miss Dempster's observation that the early part of the tale is "full of double meanings and forward allusions", asserts that "most of these further meanings come naturally to the reader, and, there is no doubt, were intended";[12] he adds to the previous list the lines

[9] Dempster, *Dramatic Irony*, pp. 49-50, footnote 91.
[10] *Ibid.*, p. 51.
[11] *Ibid.*, p. 53, footnote 108.
[12] J. S. P. Tatlock, "Chaucer's *Merchant's Tale*", *Modern Philology*, XXXIII (1936), 375-6.

which describe May as being so lovely that "Hire to biholde it semed fayerye" (1743) and says: "at once her later fairy ally Proserpina comes to mind".[13] Charles A. Owen's interest in passages within the *Canterbury Tales* which perform a symbolic and unifying function has led him to a discussion of lines 1319-36, the passage in which, he says, "the controlling images of the poem . . . the garden, the blindness, and the tree . . . are linked for the first time".[14] Although his penchant for viewing literal detail as symbol allows him interpretations which one may question as having been a part of Chaucer's intention,[15] he gives some significant indication of the way in which the images of paradise and the tree, introduced in the first portion of the tale, are given local habitation in the final scene. Similarly, in an article arguing that lyrical passages and a "generalizing impulse characteristic of allegory" offset what could be the "ruthless", "destructive" irony of the tale, J. A. Burrow discusses briefly the extended significance of these same images but concludes that their final incarnation is the "paradise" of January's "sexual fantasy realized".[16] None of these studies, however, makes full use of what the imagery of the tale reveals;[17] nor do the various discussions of the paradise motif perceive that it is inextricably linked to its opposite – hell – just as January's tardy concern for attaining heaven results directly from his fear of imminent damnation.

Even the most casual reader of the *Merchant's Tale* cannot fail to notice its violent juxtaposition of the holy and the unholy. Chaucer seems to have used every possible means of creating religious echoes to reverberate around the blatantly unmusical

---

[13]   *Ibid.*, p. 376.

[14]   Owen, "Crucial Passages in Five of the *Canterbury Tales*", p. 299.

[15]   He sees, for example, the stone wall around the garden as "the jealous precautions of the blind January as well as the inescapable unpleasantness of his love making", *ibid.*; January, bending over to encircle the pear tree with his arms, becomes "the symbol of his folly, cuckolded in the branches which spring from his head as horns", *ibid.*, p. 300.

[16]   J. A. Burrow, "Irony in the Merchant's Tale", *Anglia*, LXXV (1957), 199-208.

[17]   I am gratefully indebted to these four studies for the verification which they give in the case of this one tale to my theory of a more pervasive Chaucerian technique in the handling of imagery.

strain intoned by the stark action of his plot. On the literal level, he has the pathetically lecherous old January discuss his desired marriage in terms of the benefits it will provide for his soul (1402) and the honor it will show to "God above" (1449) and express concern lest such great earthly happiness should make him forfeit the eternal bliss of Heaven:

> For sith that verray hevene is boght so deere
> With tribulacion and greet penaunce,
> How sholde I thanne, that lyve in swich plesaunce
> As alle wedded men doon with hire wyvys,
> Come to the blisse ther Crist eterne on lyve ys?
> (1648-52)

Religious ritual is emphasized in the solemnizing of the ill-fated marriage, the priest coming forth to administer the "hooly sacrement",[18] offer prayers, and bless the pair with the sign of the Cross, thus making "al siker ynogh with hoolynesse" (1701-8). The marriage bed is likewise blessed (1819), and, as Tatlock has pointed out, Damyan's successful plea for "mercy" follows almost immediately after the celebration of a high mass (1894).[19]

The language of the tale also constantly summons up religious impressions. Upon fifty-three different occasions the name of God is invoked by the narrator or one of the various characters, either by direct reference ("The hye God, whan he hadde Adam maked", 1325), or as recipient of human prayers ("every man.../ Upon his bare knees oughte al his lyf/ Thanken his God that hym hath sent a wyf", 1350-2), or as witness for the truth of what is affirmed ("And God it woot, though I unworthy be/ I have stonden in ful greet degree", 1493-4). In like fashion, Christ is mentioned five times and the Virgin Mary three.[20] The word

---

[18] See: J. S. P. Tatlock, "The Marriage Service in Chaucer's *Merchant's Tale*", *Modern Language Notes*, XXXII (1917), 373-4; Sister Mary Immaculate, " 'Sixty' as a Conventional Number and Other Chauceriana", *Modern Language Quarterly*, II (1941), 62-3.

[19] Tatlock (note 12), p. 375. The correlating of religious observances with sensual pursuits duplicates what occurs in the *Shipman's Tale*. See pp. 116-19 above.

[20] Interestingly enough, in this tale Chaucer does not have his characters invoke any of the various saints whose names appear so frequently elsewhere in the *Canterbury Tales*. This fact would seem to emphasize the

"blisse", which is deliberately used to connote the perfection of Heaven, appears in various forms some ten times, and January himself underscores the association when he says:

> I have ... herd seyd, ful yoore ago,
> Ther may no man han parfite blisses two, –
> This is to seye, in erthe and eek in hevene.
>
> (1637-9)

Marriage is called the "holy bond", the "right of holy church", the "blessed yoke", and the "virtuous quyete", and various references are made to man's soul.

On yet another level, the reader is reminded of Biblical history by allusions to Adam and Eve, Rebecca, Judith, Abigail, Esther, Sara, and Solomon; the teachings of the early Church Fathers regarding marriage are incorporated into the discussions which make up the first half of the tale; [21] and verbal echoes from the Bible run throughout ("Goddes yifte", *Proverbs,* XIX, 14; "Passen as a shadwe", *Job,* XIV, 2),[22] climaxing, of course, as Skeat first noted, in the brilliant but devastating parody of the Song of Songs (2138-48) with which January invites May into the garden on the morning of his momentary recovery of sight.

All of these religious motifs become ironic in their discordant context, and the very act of combining the holy with a situation so sordid, though comic, creates an incongruity which deepens into profound moral criticism. Tatlock has said that "religion itself is bemocked"; [23] yet, true as this may be in one sense, the final mockery is directed not at religion but at man's distortion of its tenets. As in the *Shipman's Tale,* Chaucer offsets immorality with a solid framework of religious reference. This background establishes within the narrative itself the standard which condemns the actions of the protagonists, and from this perspective January becomes the chief offender rather than the typical dupe

---

essential nature of the religious counter-balance provided for the action of the story: its weight derives primarily from the Bible rather than Church history.

[21]   See Makarewicz (note 6).

[22]   Robinson's notes indicate all Biblical parallels.

[23]   Tatlock (note 12), p. 375.

of the fabliau. Moreover, upon several occasions Chaucer deliberately indicates through parallel construction the juxtaposition which forms the basis for his tale and contains its ultimate meaning. Nine lines from the beginning the narrator says that he knows not whether January's decision to marry were "for hoolynesse or for dotage", and this basic contradiction is made more specific by two later lines in which January contemplates "the *lusty* lyf, the *vertuous* quyete" (1395) of marriage and speaks of living in "ese and hoolynesse" (1628) once he possesses May. The most blatant example of the distortion of religious formulae comes from May herself. Having just motioned Damyan up into the pear tree and having obviously thought of the ruse which will enable her to join him there, she speaks for the first time in the narrative:

> "I have," quod she, *"a soule for to kepe*
> As wel as ye, and also myn honour,
> And of my wyfhod thilke tendre flour
> Which that I have assured in youre hond,
> Whan that *the preest to yow my body bond*;
> Wherfore I wole answere in this manere,
> By the leve of yow, my lord so deere:
> *I prey to God* that nevere dawe the day
> That I ne sterve, as foule as womman may,
> If evere I do unto my kyn that shame,
> Or elles I empeyre so my name,
> That I be fals . . .

> (2188-99)

With May, as with her counterpart in the *Shipman's Tale*, the words are merely words; they superficially echo January's concern with religious concepts but have no relation to the actions which she is about to perform. With January, the case is less simple. Although the audience has no doubts about the real motives for his marriage and the fatuity of his theological concerns, January actually seems to have convinced himself of his religious sincerity. Rather than hypocrisy, his assertions reveal yet another side of that blindness which dominates all of his reasoning and later becomes physical fact, only to be removed literally by Pluto's intervention and restored metaphorically by the combined influence of Proserpina, May, and his own refusal to see himself and his situation in the light of harsh truth. Like the merchant in the *Shipman's Tale*, January exhibits spiritual obtuseness, but its form is an inversion of the merchant's predicament. The latter, a man of noble instincts, sincerely longs for something permanent but is so submerged in materialism that he fails to see that the eternal is possible only in the realm of the spirit. January, by contrast, recognizes the existence of spiritual eternity and attempts to attain it, but the baseness of his nature permits him merely to direct his lechery to conform with the externals of the theological concept of marriage. Motivated by awareness that his life on earth must soon end ("I am hoor and oold/ And almoost, God woot, on my pittes brynke", 1400-1), he has a belated concern for his soul. He must atone for having "folwed ay his bodily delyt/ On wommen, ther as was his appetyt" (1249-50), lest he "go streight to the devel" (1436) when he dies. The method, as he sees it, is simple. By uniting himself in "holy" wedlock with a beautiful young girl, he will be carrying out a purpose "plesant to God" (1621), and the "leveful procreacioun of children" not only will prevent his heritage from falling into strange hands but will be an honor to God (1448-9). This reasoning, however sincere January may think himself to be, is mere rationalization, and although he mentions that a man should not take a wife "oonly for paramour or love" (1450), few descriptions of the sin of lust in marriage have been more graphic or repulsive than the one which Chaucer gives of him. The ultimate meaning of the *Merchant's Tale*, as of the *Shipman's Tale*, concerns spiritual blindness,[24] here made all the more fatal by a pretention to spiritual rapport, and it is for the purpose of conveying this theme that Chaucer has incorporated religious overtones on every possible level. As is the case in all of his fabliaux, however, he overtly maintains the ribaldry of the genre and allows his audience to interpret the moral significance for themselves.

[24] Many scholars have conjectured that the *Merchant's Tale* and the *Shipman's Tale*, along with the Wife of Bath's Prologue, were written at about the same time. See, for example: Tatlock, *Development and Chronology*, pp. 199-219; Brown (note 4). The similarities in structure and purpose noted herein would seem to give additional support to their conclusions.

The imagery of the tale provides yet another means of creating the basic dualism which informs the entire narrative and embodies its essential import. The first figure of speech appears in the twentieth line and is the metaphor which Chaucer apparently borrows from Deschamps but so manipulates that its significance permeates the whole tale. January, that "olde knyght, that was so wys", asserts that wedlock "in this world . . . is a paradys" (1264-5). The sarcastic note introduced by the narrator's comment on January's wisdom heralds the ironic function which this image is to perform, and because of what we know from the Prologue about the Merchant's own marital experiences, the succeeding development of the image in the long passage spoken by the narrator [25] seems deliberately and bitterly ironic.[26] Repetitions of the word "bliss" indirectly carry the image forward some fifty lines to its next appearance, where the indefinite earthly paradise is specifically equated with its Biblical original:

> The hye God, when he hadde Adam maked
> And saugh him al allone, bely-naked,
> God of his grete goodnesse seyde than,
> "Lat us now make an helpe unto this man
> Lyk to hymself"; and thanne he made him Eve.
> Heere may ye se, and heerby may ye preve,
> That wyf is mannes helpe and his confort,
> His *paradys terrestre*, and his disport.
>
> (1325-32)

Just as the later references to Biblical heroines contain deliberately ironic double meanings,[27] so this mention of Eve would im-

---

[25] Several scholars have argued that this passage is intended to represent January's thoughts. See: McGalliard (note 8); Burrow (note 16), p. 200. Appropriate as the ideas expressed might be for January, were they divested of their ironic implications, line 1393 ("For which this Januarie, of whom I tolde") would seem to indicate that Chaucer intends the passage to be the narrator's. See also: G. G. Sedgewick, "The Structure of the *Merchant's Tale*", *University of Toronto Quarterly*, XVII (1948), 341-2.

[26] For arguments that the irony is not bitter, see: Bertrand H. Bronson, "Afterthoughts on the Merchant's Tale", *Studies in Philology*, LVIII (1961), 583-96; McGalliard (note 8); Jordan (note 7).

[27] As many commentators have noted, the women mentioned all bring some sort of misfortune upon specific men: Judith cuts off Holofernes' head; Rebecca tricks the blind Isaac into blessing her favorite son, Jacob,

mediately connote to a medieval audience an interpretation opposite to that overtly stated, for in the conventional antifeminist
literature of the age she served as the archetype of womanly
frailty, the mother of man's woes, the "los of al mankynde" as
Chaucer himself phrases it in the Wife of Bath's Prologue.[28] The
narrator's irony predicts the harsh reality of January's marital
paradise, and his allusion to the Garden of Eden foreshadows
what is to be the metaphoric conclusion to the tale. The image is
repeated in the description of the wedding night:

> And Januarie hath faste in armes take
> His fresshe May, his *paradys*, his make.
>
> (1821-2)

And Chaucer, again taking a cue from Deschamps, gives the
metaphor a humorous but significant twist when he concludes the
second passage devoted to January's love-making with a terse
couplet:

> How that he wroghte, I dar nat to yow telle;
> Or wheither hire thoughte it *paradys or helle*.
>
> (1963-4)

This antithesis recalls Justinus' sensible warning to the heedless
January in the passage which contains a direct statement of the
error of January's spiritual rationalization:

> And therfore, sire ... have in youre memorie,
> Paraunter she may be youre *purgatorie*!
> She may be Goddes meene and Goddes whippe;
> Thanne shal youre soule up to hevene skippe
> Swifter than dooth an arwe out of a bowe.
> I hope to God, herafter shul ye knowe
> That ther nys no so great felicitee
> In marriage, ne nevere mo shal bee,
> *That yow shal lette of youre savacion,*

---

rather than Esau; Abigail circumvents her husband's discourtesy to David
and thus brings about Nabal's death; Esther's defense of her people results
in the death of the Persian minister, Haman; Sara's attractiveness to the
Pharaoh brings great plagues upon his house, and she later forces Abraham
to banish his son Ishmael.

[28] F. L. Utley, *The Crooked Rib* (Columbus, 1944), provides a valuable
index of English and Scottish works before 1569 which deal with the
argument about women.

> *So that ye use, as skile is and reson,*
> *The lustes of youre wyf attemprely,*
> *And that ye plese hire nat to amorously,*
> And that ye kepe yow eek from oother synne.
>
> (1668-81)

January's own ridiculous concern about the possibility that he might lose eternal paradise by enjoying the earthly paradise of marriage (1637-52) has occasioned Justinus' deliberately sarcastic reference to a wife as purgatory; yet, his warning that lust in marriage is a sin reveals the double-barrelled irony of the whole paradise-hell theme. Not only is January's vision of marital paradise to prove itself a literal hell, however blind he allows himself to remain to the fact, but his whole approach to spiritual salvation through marriage is also to damn him even more than he fears his youthful activities have, despite his ironically erroneuous assertions to May that "in oure actes we mowe do no synne./ A man may do no synne with his wyf" (1838-9).

Other images in the early part of the narrative are intimately connected to the paradise theme, and, like it, they look forward ironically to the final scene in the garden. Five lines after the first mention of paradise, the narrator says:

> ... whan a man is oold and hoor;
> Thanne is a wyf the *fruyt* of his tresor.
>
> (1269-70)

To January, May does assume the role of the choicest (the fruit) of his possessions; yet, it is later an artfully pretended desire for fruit which is to reveal just how little he actually possesses her. Moreover, as in the Garden of Eden, which the mention of Adam and Eve consciously connects with the paradise image, the fruit is symbolically linked with sin. Similarly, the early figurative references to trees become a part of the paradise complex. In January's long speech, introduced by his concern for the state of his soul, he makes the following boast about his sexual potency:

> Though I be hoor, I fare as dooth a tree
> That blosmeth er that fruyt ywoxen bee;
> And blosmy tree nys neither drye ne deed.
> I feele me nowhere hoor but on myn heed;

> Myn herte and alle my lymes been as grene
> As laurer thurgh the yeer is for the sene.
>
> (1461-66)

In terms of the action in the final scene, this comparison is ironically inept; January's obvious inability to please his wife in bed sends her scrambling up a literal tree after a metaphorical "fruit" which will be more to her taste. Because of this situation and the link which it provides with the forbidden fruit, the image of the tree itself becomes associated with the Biblical paradise. So also does January's later references to the tree of sin:

> Ther may no man han parfite blisses two, –
> This is to seye, in erthe and eek in hevene.
> For though he kepe hym fro the synnes sevene,
> And eek from *every branche of thilke tree,*
> Yet is ther so parfit felicitee
> And so greet ese and lust in mariage,
> That evere I am agast now in myn age
> That I shal lede now so myrie a lyf,
> So delicat, withouten wo and stryf,
> That I shal have myn *hevene in erthe* heere.
>
> (1638-47)

The image of the tree of sin was completely conventional in medieval theology, and Chaucer uses it in its traditional sense in the *Parson's Tale* as an introduction to the discussion of the deadly sins (X, 389). January's use of the formula here overtly refers to the conventional concept, yet this image also ironically foreshadows the final scene. D. W. Robertson has asserted that in the Middle Ages any tree may be considered as an aspect of either the Tree of Knowledge of Good and Evil responsible for the Fall or the Tree of Life, equated inevitably with the Cross, which offers man Redemption.[29] He writes:

Tropological elaborations of the two trees as trees of the virtues and vices were extremely popular in the Middle Ages. Unusually fine spe-

---

[29]   D. W. Robertson, Jr., "The Doctrine of Charity in Mediaeval Literary Gardens: A Topical Approach through Symbolism and Allegory", *Speculum*, XXVI (1951), 25.

cimens appear in the *De fructibus carnis et spiritus* printed by Migne among the works of Hugh of St. Victor. The edition in the *Patrologia* contains a schematic reproduction of the manuscript illustration which shows some of the wider implications of the trees very clearly. The evil tree on the left appears under the rubric *Vetus Adam*, or man unredeemed. The tree is rooted in *superbia* and its crowning fruit is *luxuria*. . . . The good tree on the right appears under the rubric *Novus Adam* to indicate man redeemed and in a state of grace. It is rooted in *humilitas* and its crowning fruit is *caritas* . . .[30]

This evidence would seem to suggest that the tree of sin was traditionally linked with Adam, and hence with the tree in the Garden of Eden, and thus this reference in January's speech also calls up recollections of the Biblical paradise.

Chaucer's purpose in using imagery to develop this impression of the original earthly paradise becomes evident in the final scene, where January's garden becomes an ironic and distorted reproduction of the Garden of Eden and the story of the Fall is re-enacted with equal irony. Chaucer literally embodies the whole paradise-hell theme within the details and actions of the concluding episode.

Although the beauties of January's garden are extolled at some length, the praise is couched in general terms. Only a few concrete details are given, and these parallel the equally few details of *Genesis,* II, 9-10. Like Eden, January's garden has its source of water, a "welle" (perhaps a spring) [31] rather than a river, and

---

[30] *Ibid.*, p. 26. According to Bloomfield, *Seven Deadly Sins*, p. 84, the *De fructibus*, which has been wrongly attributed to Hugh of St. Victor but dates from his period, "set the fashion for the tree image". The image was first used in connection with the sins, he says, by John Cassian (d.c. 435) in his *Collationes*, cpt. X (p. 70). The "first elaborate application of the image" appears in Boniface's poem *Aenigmata* (p. 79), and it is further developed in St. Bonaventure's *Speculum animae* (p. 89).

[31] In the *Book of the Duchess*, "welle" obviously means "spring":

> Save ther were a fewe welles
> Came rennynge fro the clyves adoun
> (160-1)

as it does in the *Troilus*:

> His eyen two, for piete of herte,
> Out stremeden as swifte welles tweye
> (IV, 246-7).

two specific trees among unnamed other varieties: a fruit and a
laurel. The relationship of the former to the Tree of the Knowledge of Good and Evil is obvious, since in both cases the plucking
of fruit by the wife results in sin – a sin, moreover, which is both
committed against the husband and yet involves him in the same
loss of Grace. The fact that the laurel is an evergreen links it
with the Tree of Life, for in the conventional medieval concept,
its leaves were depicted as evergreen to represent the unfading
and eternal Word of God.[32] Thus, the literal setting parallels the
Biblical paradise, and it is inhabited by the same erring trio: the
husband, the wife, and the tempter. Nor does Chaucer leave
Damyan's role in the final scene unexplicated, for an earlier
apostrophe has compared him specifically to a serpent:

> O perilous fyr, that in the bedstraw bredeth!
> O famulier foo, that his servyce bedeth!
> O servant traytour, false hoomly hewe,
> *Lyk to the naddre in bosom sly untrewe,*
> God shilde us alle from youre aqueyntaunce!
> O Januarie, dronken in plesaunce
> In mariage, se how thy Damyan,
> Thyn owene squier and thy borne man,
> Entendeth for to do thee vileynye.
>
> (1783-91)

Both images in this passage are ironic in terms of the situation
which January does not understand. The fire burning in the bedstraw adequately expresses the idea of the danger of having a foe
within one's own house, but because the Classical image cluster of
fire, burning, and Venus' torch as an expression of lust is used
repeatedly in the tale,[33] the image (complete with its bedstraw!)
also reveals the nature of the treachery which eventually ensues.
More important is the unoriginal simile of the snake in the bosom,
for Damyan, like the serpent in Eden, will soon urge May to
pluck the forbidden fruit. That this fruit is the act which cuckolds
January is made clear by the hypocritical excuse which May
makes for climbing the pear tree:

[32] Robertson (note 29), p. 26.
[33] See lines 1723-8, 1777, 1875-6; 1971; 2073-5.

I moste han of the peres that I see,
Or I moot dye, so soore longeth me
To eten of the smale peres grene.
Help, for hir love that is of hevene queene!
I telle yow wel, a womman in my plit
May han to fruyt so greet an *appetit*
That she may dyen, but she of if have.

(2331-7)

Her great "appetit" at this point is obviously sexual,[34] and the fact that the pears supposedly desired are green summons up ironic recollections of January's earlier boast that his heart and limbs are still green, however hoar his head (1464-6) – a boast rendered dubious by his subsequent resort to "many a letuarie" (1809). By yet another ironic twist, January's two previous mentions of trees prove equally contradictory on a different level in the denouement. January has compared himself to a laurel ever green and spoken of keeping himself from the tree of sin; yet, in the garden, the laurel or Tree of Life is completely ignored, and January obligingly embraces the tree of sin, now crowned with a very specific example of *luxuria*,[35] which has sprung from his own jealous *superbia*.

[34] Paul A. Olson, "Chaucer's Merchant and January's 'Hevene in Erthe Heere'", *English Literary History*, XXVIII (1961), 207, calls the pear tree a "phallic tree of life" and indicates in a footnote several medieval examples in which the pear is used as a phallic pun. He explains, "the pear's association with the male genitalia and with amorous affairs in general is based on the double meaning which both 'pirum' and 'poire' bear; both mean pear *and* rod" (footnote 5). Chaucer's *double-entendre* in this instance is evident, whether or not he regards the pear as a common phallic symbol.

[35] Robertson (note 29), p. 45, makes this comparison with the fruit of the tree called *Vetus Adam*. In general however, his interpretation of the garden, which is based more upon external sources than upon Chaucer's text, differs from mine. He makes such a statement as: "Ultimately, we are back at Eve and Adam's *in medio ligni paradisi*, whence the river that feeds Januarie's well runs. The 'laurer' is, in truth, 'alwey grene', for the pattern of the Fall is perennial in human experience" (p. 44). Yet, he emphasizes cupidity as January's sin rather than a presumtiveness which deems lechery holy. He says: "Januarie's garden is the garden which all those governed by cupidity think to build for self-concealment ..." (p. 45).

Alfred L. Kellogg, "Susannah and the *Merchant's Tale*", *Speculum*, XXXV (1960), 275-9, concludes his argument for an influence of medieval renderings of the story of Susannah and the elders upon Chaucer's depic-

The importance of this final scene in relation to the moral import of the tale is enhanced by its embodiment of the story of Eden. On the literal level, although the events in the garden should explode January's erroneous concept of the perfection of his marriage, his acceptance of May's explanation assures us that he will never surrender his ludicrous illusions about himself and his marriage. The significance of this self-deception in spiritual terms is conveyed through the image pattern which has here become actualized. January's spiritual blindness, and all the sins of pride, presumption and lechery which accompany it, can be remedied only by a true knowledge of good and evil which will enable him to forsake his mortally fallacious concepts. Yet, when the fruit is plucked from the tree of sin, January, unlike Adam, does not gain this knowledge. For Adam, knowledge of good and evil was sin; for January, ironically, like knowledge contains his one hope for salvation, but in his typical fashion he rejects this spiritual truth along with the gross reality of his "hevene in erthe heere". The paradise which he has hoped to achieve through marriage, here, in his garden which reproduces the earthly paradise, becomes hell; for, by his refusal to see the truth, he damns

tion of January's garden with yet another interpretation of the garden. He points out that the "sponsa" of the Song of Songs, sacrilegiously parodied by January, was variously understood in the Middle Ages as the Church, the individual soul, and the Virgin Mary, and that "hortus conclusus", an epithet for the chaste "sponsa", was often used in hymns to describe the Virgin. January's garden is also enclosed. Thus, he finds in this final scene a juxtaposition of "the image of supremely chaste love – the 'hortus conclusus' with its inescapable Marian overtones, and the image of supremely unchaste love – the doubled unnatural lust of the elders" (p. 278). "As by a series of mirrors" he concludes, "the moral distortion of old January is brought before the reader's eyes, and none reveals him more fully than that which presents a doubled image of January's lust set against the highest love the Middle Ages could conceive" (p. 279). His arguments for an indirect association of the garden with the Virgin Mary seem plausible, although I do not think that this is the primary "doubled image" apparent in the garden. I might add that two of the three direct references in the tale to the Virgin occur in the garden scene.

Olson (note 34), pp. 203-14, discusses both the Garden of Eden associations and those arising from the Song of Songs to support his idea of January's sin of avarice. "This is only a mimic fall in a mimic bourgeois paradise", he writes (p. 213).

himself completely. Thus, the early development of the paradise-
hell image proves ironically true; and, as if to underscore this
fact in concrete terms, Chaucer chooses for his interfering divini-
ties Pluto and Proserpina, who, however metamorphosed they
are into the medieval king and queen of fairy,[36] are nonetheless
the traditional rulers of Hades.[37] Hell exists in paradise on every
level in this final scene – all in order to demonstrate the moral
purpose which informs the whole tale.

In addition to this major image pattern which contributes so
significantly to the ultimate meaning of the tale, Chaucer also
introduces incidental figurative clusters which function ironically
in relation to various elements of the plot. For example, when
January mistakenly assures May that a man may do no sin with
his wife, he adds: "Ne hurte hymselven with his owene knyf"
(1840). Later, when he invites May into the garden, he says,
speaking of his passion for her: "Thou hast me *wounded* in myn
herte" (2145), and a few lines later he asserts:

> For by that Lord that sit in hevene above,
> Levere ich hadde *to dyen on a knyf*,
> Than thee offende, trewe deere wyf!
>
> (2162-4)

Climaxing these references, he says as he stoops down for her to
climb from his back into the pear tree and the arms of Damyan:

> "Certes . . . thereon shal be no lak,
> Mighte I yow helpen *with myn herte blood*."
>
> (2346-7)

One of the few specific things which Chaucer tells us about
Damyan is that he "*carf* biforn the knyght ful many a day"
(1773),[38] and in this final scene, by a kind of ironic synecdoche,

---

[36] Bronson (note 26), pp. 593-4, discusses this point and denies, rightly it
seems to me, a dark, sinister characterization of Pluto and Proserpina.
Nonetheless, Chaucer and his audience knew who they were in Classical
mythology.

[37] Mortimer J. Donovan, "The Image of Pluto and Proserpine in the
Merchant's Tale", *Philological Quarterly*, XXXVI (1957), 49-60, points out
various parellels between January and Pluto, such as the fact that both
are old men with young wives.

[38] Owen (note 14), p. 299, points out the relationship of line 1773 to
line 1840.

he is indeed the knife, January's "owene knyf", destined to prove
the falsity of the old man's initial sententious utterance. The
wound which he inflicts as he makes January a cuckold results
from the same sexual source as does the wound which January
sentimentally ascribes to himself in line 2145, and the heart's
blood which is drawn should, were not the victim so wilfully
deceived, cause the death which January has said he would rather
suffer than offend May. Unrecognized as the fact remains to him,
January does "die on a knife" precisely because he IS offensive
to May.

Similarly, when commenting upon May's reaction to the wedding festivities, Chaucer employs a simile so oft-used as to be
almost meaningless: "The bryde was broghte abedde *as stille as
stoon*" (1818); yet, by later repetitions, even this utterly conventional image gains ironic significance. Her lack of response
January regards as maidenly modesty ("Allas! I moot trespace/
To yow, my spouse", 1828-9), but because he is "as *blynd as is a
stoon*" (2156) even before his physical loss of sight, he thus mis-
interprets the situation. With Damyan, however, because she is
not one of those women "That hath an herte *as hard as any
stoon*" (1990), her reaction is both immediate and positive.

In Placebo's major speech, one incidental image occurs which
has occasioned scholars some difficulty. While voicing his completely meaningless approval of January's plan to wed a young
wife, the flatterer says: "Youre herte hangeth on a joly pyn!"
(1516). Skeat explained this phrase as meaning "your heart is in
a merry state". He writes:

A *pin* was a name for a wooden peg; and *to hang on a pin* was to be
hung up conspicuously. Palsgrave, p. 844, has: 'Upon a mery pynne,
de hayt; as *il a la cueur de hayt*'; cf. '*Hait*, liveliness. . . . cheerfulness'
in Cotgrave. Halliwell gives: '*on the pin*, on the *qui vive*.' Later, the
phrase became *in a merry pin*, i.e. in a good humour; but this is
thought to refer to the pins or pegs in a 'peg-tankard'; see *Pin* in
Nares. Cowper, in his John Gilpin, has 'in merry pin.'[39]

Klaeber repeats this interpretation, but confesses that the significance of the phrase is not very clear to him:

[39]   W. W. Skeat, ed., *The Works of Geoffrey Chaucer, V*, 358.

Einer besonderen Form der Wendung; 'to be in a merry pin' begegnen wir in dem Ausdruck: *Your herte hongith on a joly pyn* ... ; doch ist mir die dieser Form zu Grunde liegende Vorstellung nicht recht klar.[40]

It seems to me that Chaucer surely intended this to be a pun similar to the "score it upon my taille" of the *Shipman's Tale*. In Old French as in modern, "pine" was a crude term for the male sexual organ. Godefroy defines it as "membre viril – N'est plus employé que dans un langage grossier."[41] With this double meaning, which Chaucer and his audience would undoubtedly know, the phrase becomes ironically meaningful in a typically Chaucerian way. Placebo, who intends only to second all of January's overt arguments in favor of the marriage, unwittingly states the true motive for the plan and reveals the flaw in the old man's spiritual rationalization: the only "heart" which enters into the situation does indeed "hang" upon mere lust.

The gross sensuality of January's idea of a "leveful" love which will save his soul is also emphasized by a series of food images:

> I wol noon oold wyf han in no manere.
> She shal nat passe twenty yeer, certayn;
> Oold fissh and yong flessh wolde I have ful fayn.
> Bet is," quod he, "a pyk than a pykerel,
> And bet than old boef is the tendre veel.
> I wol no womman thritty yeer of age;
> It is but bene-straw and greet forage.
>
> (1416-22)

These references relate ironically to the statement that "appetyt" (1250) has caused the promiscuity for which he now believes he must atone, and the parallel thus created through imagery further reveals the falsity of his spiritual rationalization. Moreover, just as January is confused by the nature of his own "appetite", so he is deceived in the garden about May's appetite, which despite its overt and implied meanings is nonetheless, as noted above, merely sexual.

[40] Klaeber, *Das Bild bei Chaucer*, p. 421.
[41] Frederic Godefroy, *Dictionnaire de l'ancienne langue française*, VI (Paris, 1889), 165.

Various comparisons of January to animals also echo an early statement: namely, that bachelors, whose love is not devoted to one woman, live "but as a bryd or as a beest/ In libertee" (1281-2). Through similes, the sexual license of the animal world re-appears in January, who is described on his wedding night as a dogfish (1825), a colt (1847), and a "flekked pye" (1848), and Chaucer concludes the distressing scene with a reference which makes the association clear:

> For every labour somtyme moot han reste,
> Or elles longe may he nat endure;
> This is to seyn, no lyves creature,
> Be it of fyssh, or bryd, or beest, or man.
>
> (1862-5)

Later, in the garden where the "thynges whiche that were nat doon abedde" are "parfourned" and "spedde" (2051-2), January – unaware of the intruders, human and divine – "syngeth ful murier than the papejay" (2322). His light-heartedness here, as in the previous scene, is connected with sex, and the assertion which he makes immediately after the comparison to the parrot – "Yow love I best, and shal, and oother noon" (2323) – suffers from the juxtaposition. Not only are we reminded of the animal instinct which has prompted this infatuation, but also, as in the *Shipman's Tale*, the parrot's stupidity in learning to imitate human speech [42] offers ironic commentary upon January's stupidity in his attempt to imitate a marriage "pleasant to God".

Damyan and May also receive their due share of ironic animal associations. When the former miraculously recovers from his illness, having been effectively dosed by May's acquiescent letter, he goes to January "as lowe/ As evere dide a dogge for the bowe" (2013-4). The image gives a graphic impression of his hypo-critical humility, but it also reveals the true situation: for the hunting dog, the game is almost caught; the wounded deer is within sight. May, on the other hand, is hopefully compared to a turtle-dove by January. Consumed with jealousy after he loses his sight, he cannot endure the thought that she may have another lover after he dies; she must "evere lyve as wydwe in clothes

42   See p. 115 above.

blake,/ Soul as the turtle that lost hath hire make" (2079-80). So greatly does he desire such faithfulness that he even asserts its existence; when he invites May into the garden, he says, using a phrase from the Song of Songs but redirecting its meaning:

> "Rys up, my wyf, my love, my lady free!
> The turtles voys is herd, *my dowve sweete* . . .
> (2138-9)

The irony of this image is devastating, for May proceeds not only to negate its symbolic appropriateness by the grossest of infidelity but also to verify its biological aptness by selecting a tree as the spot for the illicit act.

One additional animal image, inserted by the narrator as an apostrophe to Fortune, has an ironic relationship to both Damyan and May. When reporting that January has literally gone blind, the narrator exclaims:

> O sodeyn hap! o thou Fortune unstable!
> Lyk to the scorpion so deceyvable,
> That flaterest with thyn heed whan thou wolt stynge;
> Thy tayl is deeth, thurgh thyn envenymynge.
> O brotil joye! o sweete venym queynte!
> O monstre, that so subtilly kanst peynte
> Thy yiftes under hewe of stidefastnesse,
> That thou deceyvest bothe moore and lesse!
> (2057-64)

Although overtly linked to Fortune and connected with January's physical loss of sight, this comparison to the scorpion far better suits the hypocrisy being practised by May and her lover. Both "flatter" old January "under hewe of stidefastnesse" while planning to "stynge" him in a way inevitably related to "tayls".[43] As is frequently the case in Chaucer's fabliaux, this latter word has sexual implications,[44] which are here underscored by the "queynte" of the next line. Although ostensibly an adjective, "queynte" as a noun states the actual truth: [45] January finds May's sexual com-

[43]   In the fourth part of the *Ancren Riwle*, the scorpion is equated with the sin of lechery. Chaucer, however, uses the same image in two other places to express mere deceitfulness without any ironic *double-entendre*. See: *B. of the D.*, 636-41; *Man of Law's T.*, II, 404-6.

[44]   See Cpt. V, p. 92 and footnote 7 above; Cpt. VI, p. 108 and footnote 8.

[45]   Baum, "Chaucer's Puns", p. 243, lists this use of "queynte" as a pun.

pliance "sweet", but he is about to have an opportunity to realize
that it is also "venom" to him. By a further ironic twist, however,
the very "stynge" which should be "deeth" to his illusions serves
instead to restore his physical sight.

If the foregoing analysis has the validity which the patterns of
imagery and the extensive framework of religious reference within
the tale seem to provide, then the image which Chaucer here repeats from both the *Shipman's Tale* and the *Parson's Tale* ironically
sums up the whole theme. When the narrator states that a wife is
a gift which will last while all other possessions "passen as a
shadwe upon a wal" (1311-18), his distortion of the Biblical
phrase is indicated by his sour conclusion:

> A wyf wol laste, and in thyn hous endure,
> Wel lenger than thee list, paraventure.

(1317-18)

Yet, this traditional reminder of the illusiveness of worldly things
ironically foreshadows January's predicament, both earthly and
spiritual. His inability to distinguish on any level the difference
between illusion and reality is not only the characteristic which
motivates the entire plot but is also the ultimate flaw which
condemns him, both as dupe of the fabliau and as mortal sinner
of the covert moral exemplum.

As was the case with the *Shipman's Tale*, it is obvious that the
moral implications of the narrative are not appropriate sentiments
for the pilgrim to whom the story is ascribed. Much has been
written about the subtle dramatic fitness of this tale in relation to
the Merchant, and I would certainly not want to deny any of
these observations. I would suggest, however, that since Chaucer
apparently composed the tale before he wrote the Merchant's
Prologue,[46] he framed the story to suit his own purposes and later
provided only such dramatic suitability between tale and teller as
would adequately serve his general scheme. The bitterness of this
tale is not Chaucer's, we have been frequently told – perhaps
not, if in fact it is bitter; but the moral lesson and the artistry
which has given the tale its ultimate meaning are indeed Chaucer's.

---

[46]   See: Tatlock (note 24), pp. 200-1; Brown (note 4), p. 1044; Bronson
(note 26), p. 584 ff.

VIII

THE SUMMONER'S TALE

In commenting upon Jacques de Baisieux' *Li Dis de Vescie a Prestre*, which is the only recorded analogue of the *Summoner's Tale*, Walter Morris Hart has praised both its unique development of the character of the sick man and its effective use of irony. He conjectures, however, that Chaucer was not familiar with the early fourteenth-century fabliau, since his own tale does not duplicate its artistry:

... had he encountered the character of the Priest, had his attention been called to the possibilities for irony in speech and situation, he would surely have developed them in the *Summoner's Tale*, as he had developed similar matters in the *Friar's Tale*. But he had other fish to fry: the Summoner must tell a tale at the expense of a Friar; the character of the Friar must then be the important matter, not the plot, not the character of the sick man; and not irony, which, in any case, had just been exploited in the *Friar's Tale*.[1]

One can hardly disagree that the character of the friar and his humiliation are the major concerns of the Summoner, but, as two more recent critics, Earle Birney and John F. Adams, have pointed out,[2] to deny the importance of irony in the tale is to overlook a curiously insistent feature of its first 450 lines. Even the basic outlines of the plot are, of course, ironic: the begging friar who anticipates a gift of gold receives instead a ludicrous insult, and when he complains to the lord and seeks redress for this affront, he gains only further mortification. This essential irony is

---

[1] Bryan and Dempster, pp. 276-7.
[2] Earle Birney, "Structural Irony with the Summoner's Tale", *Anglia*, LXXVIII (1960), 204-18; John F. Adams, "The Structure of Irony in *The Summoner's Tale*", *Essays in Criticism*, XII (1962), 126-32.

deepened by the brilliant characterization of the friar which Chaucer sets forth in the first half of the tale, for the more greedy, glib, and self-satisfied the hypocrite,[3] the more ridiculous the frustration of his aspirations. But this portrayal is not the only ironic purpose which Chaucer has for the first part of his narrative. In a manner similar to that of the *Merchant's Tale*, although less complex, he so manipulates the friar's dialogue that the victim unwittingly forecasts his own downfall. The following analysis must of necessity repeat some specific observations already made by Professors Birney and Adams, because in both the foreshadowing process and the exposure of the friar's character, imagery interacting with specific detail once again serves to augment the irony established by other means.

The friar's hypocrisy is neatly revealed in the introductory portion of the tale so that his later discussion with Thomas is colored by what we already know about the character of the protagonist. He successfully exhorts the people in church to give money to his order rather than to the beneficed clergy or the rival monasteries, where it will be "wasted and devoured" (1720) by the "possessioners" who live in "wele and habundaunce" (1723); however, we see him, immediately thereafter, "pouring and prying" into every house, begging for precisely such "habundaunce" as may literally be "devoured" (wheat, malt, rye, cheese, etc.), writing down the names of those who contribute so that he may later pray for them, and then scraping the names off the ivory tablet as soon as he is again out of doors. As a result of these initial scenes, his first words to Thomas become ironically significant:

> "Thomas," quod he, "God yelde yow! ful ofte
> Have I upon this bench faren ful weel;
> Heere have I *eten many a myrie meel*."
>
> (1772-4)

Then, when asked where he has been the past fortnight, he replies:

[3] For an account of the ways in which Chaucer's friars reflect the typical charges brought against the orders in the thirteenth and fourteenth centuries, see: Arnold Williams, "Chaucer and the Friars", *Speculum*, XXVIII (1953), 499-513.

"God woot . . . laboured have I ful soore,
And specially, for they savacion
Have I *seyd many a precious orison*,
And for oure othere freendes, God hem blesse!

(1784-7)

The climax to this sort of pretended concern for the spiritual
welfare of donors comes when he asserts to Thomas' wife that he
had a miraculous vision of her child, who died two weeks before,
being carried to Heaven. He carefully states that no bells were
rung on the occasion, however, so that his tale cannot be denied
by anyone who might have been near his convent at the time
this miracle supposedly occurred.[4]

In his sermonistic lecture to Thomas after the wife's departure,
the friar repeatedly emphasizes the poverty and abstinence of his
brotherhood and condemns the gluttony of other religious orders:

Fy on hire pompe and on hire glotonye!
And for hir lewednesse I hem diffye.
   Me thynketh they been lyk Jovinyan,
Fat as a whale, and walkynge as a swan,
Al vinolent as botel in the spence.

(1927-31)

Although the point of his discourse is that the fasting and humility of the friars make their prayers more efficacious, all of this
talk is merely his circuitous way of leading up to the request for
money, however incongruous such a demand may be after his
extolling of the humble friars "wedded to poverte". His diatribe
against gluttony, moreover, is rendered equally hollow by his
amusing instructions to the wife to prepare him only the choicest
morsels for dinner:

Have I nat of a capon but the lyvere,
And of youre softe breed nat but a shyvere,
And after that a rosted pigges heed –
But that I nolde no beest for me were deed –
Thanne hadde I with yow hoomly suffisaunce.
I am a man of litel sustenaunce;
My spirit hath his fostryng in the Bible.

[4]   This point was first made by John S. P. Tatlock, "Notes on Chaucer:
The Canterbury Tales", *Modern Language Notes*, XXIX (1914), 144.

> The body is ay so redy and penyble
> To wake, that my stomak is destroyed.
>
> (1839-47)

This aspect of his hypocrisy is reinforced by two images which he uses when describing his supposed virtues and the special effectiveness of his order. The prayers of "charitable and chaste bisy freres", he says, rise directly up to God's ears, "right as an *hauk* up at a sours/ Up springeth into th'eir" (1938-9). His choice of bird for this comparison is an ironic revelation of his true nature, for the hawk is a notorious bird of prey, just as is this particular friar, although he goes to great lengths to mask his rapaciousness under smooth, self-asserted humility. Earlier, he speaks of devoting all his time to "fishing" for men's souls (1820), and once again, although this is a well-known Biblical image, it has an added ironic implication in relation to the friar, who certainly does spend all his energies on fishing, not for souls, but for the usual non-metaphoric results: food.

He also repeatedly extolls the chastity of friars, but his own greeting to the wife displays a sensuality hardly in accord with his words on the subject:

> The frere ariseth up ful curteisly,
> And hire embraceth in his armes narwe,
> And kiste hire sweete, and chirketh as a sparwe
> With his lyppes: "Dame," quod he, "right weel
> As he that is youre servant every deel,
> Thanked be God, that yow yaf soule and lyf!
> Yet saught I nat this day so fair a wyf
> In al the chirche, God so save me!"
>
> (1802-9)

Chaucer makes his ironic intention in this passage clear by the comparison to a sparrow, a bird traditionally associated with lechery and so used in the poet's portrait of the teller of this tale (*Gen. Pro.*, 626).

In similar fashion the Friar's preaching against ire is negated by his own actions. He is motivated to lecture to Thomas about this sin because the wife has initially complained about her sick husband's bad temper – surely an understandable reaction to the situation she describes from a man who is ill:

"Chideth him weel, for seinte Trinitee!
He is as angry as a pissemyre,
Though that he have al that he kan desire.
Though I hym wrye a-nyght and make hym warm,
And over hym leye my leg outher myn arm,
He groneth lyk oure boor, lith in oure sty,
Oother desport right noon of hym have I!
I may nat plese hym in no maner cas."

(1824-31)

The friar begins his little sermon with the statement "Ye lye heere ful of anger and of ire/ With which the devel *set youre herte afyre*" (1981-2), thus misinterpreting the cause of Thomas' peevishness just as the wife has rather stupidly done, and he goes on to exhort Thomas to be "no leon" in his house (1989). The figurative comparisons used in these speeches gain ironic importance when the friar concludes his lecture on ire with insistent pleas that Thomas confess himself and contribute to the order's cloister-building fund. The sick man becomes truly angered by the friar's "false dissymulacioun": he "wax wel ny wood for ire;/ He wolde that the frere had been on-fire" (2121-2). It is precisely with this repetition of the fire image that Thomas decides to give the friar a gift of the physical reality which he HAS been lying there full of and which is no doubt symptomatic of his illness, the cause of his previously misunderstood temper. Once the "gift" is bestowed, the friar forgets all his moral advice, starts up "as dooth a wood leoun" (2152), and rushes forth with a "ful angry cheere":

He looked as it were a wilde boor;
He grynte with his teeth, so was he wrooth.

(2160-1)

Through repetition of the animal similes, Chaucer underscores the irony of the whole episode. Thomas' initial "ire" is classified as the fretfulness it really is by the pettiness of the comparisons to an ant and to a tame boar grunting in its sty, but the friar mistakenly assesses it as the ferocity of a lion and delivers a completely unjustified sermon. Then, he himself displays the very ire which he has just condemned by behaving both like a lion and like a wild, rather than a tame boar. "Ire is a synne, oon of the grete of sevene,/ Abhomynable unto the God of hevene;/ And to hymself it is destruccion" (2005-7), the friar has earlier said; now, as he rushes forth to the lord's house in the clutches of that very sin, he is about to experience the truth of his sententiousness in a ridiculous but effective way.

The lecture which the friar gives to Thomas also performs another ironic function within the tale. As he holds forth upon the superiority of friars and the evils of gluttony and ire and repeatedly twists his discourse back to the subject of the desired donation, he unconsciously predicts both the nature of the "cherles dede" and the further humiliation which he receives when he makes his complaint to the lord. In the case of the latter, the two *exempla* which Chaucer has him include in his sermon on ire seem to have been chosen precisely for their ironic relationship to the concluding scene. The first of these anecdotes, from Seneca's *De ira*, tells of a judge who, upon being asked to dispense justice to a knight erroneously suspected of murdering a companion, condemns him to death, and who then, when the charge is found to be a mistake and the sentence thus unjustified, refuses to alter his verdict but instead, upon its basis, condemns also the companion and the man instructed to carry out the first death sentence. This inversion of justice foreshadows what is to occur to the friar when he complains to the lord; by telling his tale, he gains no amends for the insult offered him but merely succeeds in making himself and his brother friars the objects of humiliating laughter, completely undeserved from his point of view. The second *exemplum* is itself ironic. A sincere counsellor warns Cambises of the dangers of drink, and as a result, to prove that the advice is wrong and that drink has neither palsied his hand nor bleared his eyesight, Cambises shoots an arrow through the heart of the counsellor's young son. The tale is ironically linked to the final scene, however, by the self-revealing interpretation which the friar gives to it. Although supposedly preaching against ire, he draws a moral which again exposes his hypocrisy:

> Beth war, therfore, with lordes how ye pleye.
> Syngeth *Placebo*, and 'I shal, if I kan,'

But if it be unto a povre man.
To a povre man men sholde his vices telle,
But nat to a lord, though he sholde go to helle.

                                            (2074-8)

What the friar means, of course, is that one should not tell a
lord about the lord's vices,[5] but by an ironic twist of this hypocritical advice, his own final humiliation comes because he has
failed to beware of how he "pleyes" with a lord, has failed to
take heed of what he reveals of HIS OWN vices. Both in his sermon
at the church and in what he tells of his interview with Thomas,
he has disclosed his own falsity, as Jankyn's concluding sarcastic
words make evident:

The worthy men of hem shul first be served;
And certeinly he hath it weel disserved.
He hath to-day taught us so muche good
With prechyng in the pulpit ther he stood,
That I may vouche sauf, I sey for me,
He hadde the firste smel of fartes thre;
And so wolde al his covent hardily,
He bereth hym so faire and hoolily.

                                            (2279-86)

Similarly, two other things which the friar innocently says to
Thomas anticipate the final scene. Concluding his sermon on ire
and urging the sick man to confess himself, he says:

Now, Thomas, leeve brother, lef thyn ire;
Thou shalt me fynde as just as is a squyre.
Hoold nat the develes knyf ay at thyn herte –
Thyn angre dooth thee al to soore smerte –

                                            (2089-92)

The reference to the justice of a squire (an example of the rhetorical *imago*) and the metaphor of ire as the devil's knife are ironically enacted at the lord's house. In this scene Jankyn plays the

---

[5] A similar statement concludes the anecdote in Seneca's *De ira*: "Acces-
sit itaque ad numerum eorum, qui magnis cladibus ostenderunt, quanti
constarent regum amicis bona consilia" (Bryan and Dempster, p. 287). In
this context, however, the assertion is deliberate sarcasm. When Chaucer
adapts the passage to the hypocritical friar, he expands the idea and
eliminates the sarcasm by having what is said precisely suit the character
of the speaker.

major role, and we are told only two facts about him: that he is the lord's squire and that he carves the lord's meat (2243-4). When the lord mock-seriously ponders the problem in "ars-metrike" (2222) [6] posed by Thomas' "gift", it is the squire who solves the question of equal division and provides a facetious means for just distribution of the fart. With a skill surely equal to that required by his customary duty, he thus wields the "develes knyf" provided by the friar's own anger so that it indeed causes the latter "al to soore smerte". Perhaps even more explicit in its ironic duplication is the friar's earlier remark to Thomas:

> What is a ferthyng worth parted in twelve?
> Lo, ech thyng that is oned in himselve
> Is moore strong than whan it is toscatered.
>
> (1967-9)

By this pun,[7] which the friar certainly does not intend but Chaucer obviously does, we are forewarned of the final image of the cartwheel with its twelve spokes (2255-7), which is proposed to insure equitable scattering of something "strong", and which Jankyn describes with all the visual clarity of the rhetorical *demonstratio*.

Equally unfortunate choices of subject matter and phrasing in the friar's lecture likewise anticipate the nature of Thomas' gift,

[6]   Baum, "Chaucer's Puns", p. 231, notes the obvious double meaning of "ars-metrike". The modern reader is also tempted to see an unwitting pun when the friar earlier says to Thomas:
> What nedeth yow diverse freres seche?
> What nedeth hym that hath a *parfit leche*
> To sechen othere leches in the toun?
>
> (1955-7)
Although the friar is here using "leche" in its customary ME sense of "physician", the figurative meaning as "one who stick to someone else for motives of gain" is too perfect a description of the true character of the friar to escape notice. Unfortunately however, the earliest reference given by the *NED* to "leech" in this figurative sense is from Cowper's *Task* (1784). Of course, the leech as a blood-sucking animal appears in OE texts (e.g. Proverbs of AElfred, #472, in the *OE Miscellany*), and it is at least possible that Chaucer might here be punning on the blood-sucker, giving it the metaphoric humanization which later became standard usage.

[7]   J. Edwin Whitesell' "Chaucer's Lisping Friar", *Modern Language Notes*, LXXI (1956), 160-1, in noting the significance of this line, argues that if the friar in the tale lisps as does the pilgrim being insulted, the comment suggested the crude joke to Thomas.

if they do not indeed actually provide him with the idea. Because Chaucer allows Thomas only three remarks during the long course of the friar's verbosity, the tale does not really justify this latter interpretation. Yet, we know that from the beginning Thomas has very decided doubts about the value of giving money to friars (1948-54) and may assume that he has begun to recognize the hypocrite for what he is. By the end of the sermon, we know that this suspicion has grown into violent conviction, and it is therefore tempting to picture him disgruntledly construing from the friar's own words the kind of donation appropriate to bestow and being prompted to a vindictive, ironically fitting action by the *exemplum* of Cambises' vindictiveness. Be that as it may however, what the friar says has obviously been manipulated to foreshadow the crude "donation" just as it does the final scene.

The description of gluttony – which must surely serve as an untimely reminder of the sick man's present alimentary difficulties – leads the friar to the subject of digestive bodily functions as he sneeringly puns on the Latin *eructare* (literally, "to belch"; figuratively, "to talk of", "to emit").[8] He depicts his favorite whipping boys, the "possessioners", as being so replete in their over-indulgence that they recite the "psalm of Davit" (Ps. xliv, 2: "Eructavit cor meum verbum bonum") with indecorous sound effects:

> Hir preyere is of ful greet reverence,
> Whan they for soules seye the psalm of Davit;
> Lo, 'buf!' they seye, '*cor meum eructavit*!'
>
> (1932-4)

A later unintentional pun brings the matter even closer to what Thomas decides to do. Just twenty lines before Thomas makes up his mind, the friar pleads for gold for the unfinished cloister and asserts: "God woot, unnethe the fundement/ Parfourned is" (2103-4). Ironically, the response to this plea is a "gift" directly connected with the fundament but "unnethe" that! [9] Moreover,

[8] Paul Beichner, "Non Alleluia Ructare", *Mediaeval Studies*, XVIII (1956), 135-44, discusses this pun at length and argues that no medieval audience could fail to catch the significance.

[9] The pun on "fundement" is listed by Baum (note 6), p. 237. Chaucer uses "fundement" to mean "anus" in the Host's comments to the Pardoner at the end of the latter's tale (*Pard. T.*, 950).

when responding to Thomas' initial complaint that all the money
he has given has been merely wasted, the friar comes forth with
another unfortunate *sententia*:

> Thomas, of me thou shalt nat been yflattered;
> Thou woldest han oure labour al for noght.
> The hye God, that al this world hath wroght,
> Seith that the werkman worthy is his hyre.
>
> (1970-3)

As far as Thomas can see, and as we know to be the truth, this
particular "workman" has produced nothing but a lot of pious
talk; thus, by an inversion of his own proverb, it is most fitting
that the friar's hot air be paid in like token.

When the friar's actions and speeches are viewed in this light,
then an early, seemingly innocuous statement which he makes
becomes an ironic foreshadowing of his exact fate. In talking
about the sermon which he has given that day, he asserts that it
is not his practice to use the verbatim "text of hooly writ" because it is too hard for a layman to understand; he instead teaches
"al the glose". He concludes this self-satisfied comment with:

> *Glosynge* is a glorious thyng, certeyn,
> For *lettre sleeth*, so as we clerkes seyn.
>
> (1793-4)

Although he uses "glosynge" here to mean "explanation", the
alternate meaning of "cajolery" or "wheedling" is a far more
appropriate statement of what this hypocrite truly venerates; and
it is when this same wheedling angers Thomas that the exact
letter of the friar's words are enacted with a physical concreteness
which certainly "sleeth" his pride. Similar in its later ironic physical embodiment is the verb which the friar metaphorically uses
for spiritual matters when he complains that curates are "ful
necligent and slowe/ To *grope* tendrely a conscience/ In shrift"
(1816-18). This key word, which here describes the religious duty
that the friar constantly asserts is the special achievement of men
of his order, reappears twice, in what might be considered a use
of the rhetorical *traductio*, when Thomas makes his final offer
("put in thyn hand doun by my bak"/ ... "and *grope* wel
bihynde" – 2140-1) and the friar eagerly follows the instructions

("Aboute his tuwel *grope* there and heere" – 2148). With unerring accuracy, Chaucer deflates the friar's meaningless assertions of spiritual superiority by showing to what vulgar and ludicrous lengths his true "groping" is willing to go.

Despite Professor Hart's assertion, then, the *Summoner's Tale*, Chaucer's one adaption of the scatological fabliau, depends upon irony for its effect in much the same measure as do his tales which hinge primarily upon sexuality. Moreover, the role which imagery plays in creating this irony also corresponds to his technique in the other fabliaux, the rhetorical figures interacting with narrative detail in such a way that they extend their significance beyond their immediate context. The resultant irony, however, is typically Chaucerian: it owes nothing to the French analogue. Jacques de Baisieux creates a delightful but simple irony of situation by having a day elapse between the dying priest's promise that he will give the friars a "jewel" and the revelation that this gift is really his bladder. In the interval the friars celebrate their good fortune with drunken revelry, feasting and ringing the cloister bells so wildly that people think some miracle has occurred. When they arrive early the next day to collect their gift, the priest has them summon all the town officials to witness the presentation, thus plotting to expose the friars to the ridicule and humiliation which they deserve. The gift itself, however, has no ironic relevance to the friars' previous begging, and the only irony of speech in the tale appears in what the priest says at the moment when he reveals the nature of the "jewel":

> Si ai pensé si longement
> K'apenseis me sui d'une coze
> Ke j'ai *en mon porpris encloze,*
> Ke *j'aime mut et tieng mut chiere,*
> Mais je lor doin en tel maniere
> *K'ilh ne l'aront tant con vivrai,*
> Car onkes ne le delivrai
> En autrui garde k'en la moie.
> Sachiés ke durement l'amoie
> Et *amerai tote ma vie*:
> Sans convoitise et sans envie
> Lor done chi en vo presence.   (272-83) [10]

[10]   Bryan and Dempster, p. 285.

Chaucer's irony is far more subtle, and the purpose it serves is essentially more serious, even though his fabliau is much more vulgar than *Li Dis de Vescie a Prestre*.

The final question, of course, is precisely that: for what purpose has Chaucer expended such careful artistry upon his tale? What does he ultimately achieve by manipulating metaphor, simile, *imago*, and *demonstratio* – along with such other rhetorical figures as *traductio, adnominatio* or pun, *sententia*, and *exemplum* – so that they all have an ironic relationship to the progression of the narrative? The motive is surely, in part, sheer fun; but, on quite another level, the technique deepens the poetic justice of the tale. Hypocrisy is not only punished; it fails because of its integral flaw – and this fact, which the true assessment of the friar's character made by Thomas and the lord's household illustrates in one way, is rendered concrete by the friar's unconscious foreshadowing of his own humiliation. His whole existence exemplifies talk which has no relationship to deed, and when two gross actions derived from his talk are actually performed, the very nature of his falsity cannot endure the mortifying example of the morally correct correspondence of word to deed.

IX

THE MILLER'S TALE

Almost without exception, every modern critic who has chosen to discuss the *Miller's Tale* has asserted that this ribald farce is a supreme achievement of Chaucer's art. E. M. W. Tillyard, for example, declares that "it is the most brilliantly plotted of all the *Tales* and the character-sketches in no way yield to those of the Prologue"; [1] John Livingston Lowes avows that "for pure virtuosity" it is perhaps Chaucer's "masterpiece"; [2] E. T. Donaldson describes it as "the highest artistic expression of the fabliau", [3] Charles Muscatine as "the fabliau at the stage of richest elaboration". [4] Even R. K. Root, who thought it "unfortunate" that Chaucer had included such bawdy narratives in his collection, could not but admire what he found distasteful: "In none of Chaucer's tales is there more convincing proof of his mastery of the technique of story telling." [5]

Singled out as bases for such acclaim have been the subtleness of the parallel which the tale provides for the Knight's courtly romance, the vividness and economy of the characterization, the close interweaving of setting and action, the high-spiritedness of the comedy, the development of action from character, the crude but effective poetic justice, the mathematical perfection of the plot culminating in the flawless bit of timing which unites in one hilarious moment the two themes previously developed, and the resultant sense of inevitability which seems to give the tale a

[1]   E. M. W. Tillyard, *Poetry Direct and Oblique* (London, 1948), p. 215.
[2]   Lowes, *Geoffrey Chaucer*, pp. 222-3.
[3]   Donaldson, *Chaucer's Poetry*, p. 906.
[4]   Muscatine, *French Tradition*, p. 224.
[5]   Root, *Poetry of Chaucer*, pp. 176-7.

philosophical depth hardly to be anticipated from a train of action overtly so crude and farcical. Professor Muscatine has described the latter as "an assertion of the binding, practical sequentiality of all events",[6] and he has pointed out that Chaucer so uses details within the narrative, that either by "antecedents or consequences", they account for everything which occurs:

The very smallest scraps of image and action are handled ... consequentially, even where they are entirely unnecessary to the gross plot. ... The whole denouement, coming when it does, is by virtue of a mass recurrence of images given an air of utter probability. The nocturnal visit of Absolon to the carpenter's house has first a dress rehearsal that seems inconsequential ... except to familiarize us with this action, with such details as the wall and the hinged window, and with such minute facts as that the window can be heard through. ... Similarly, the cockcrow, the knocking, the (sweetsmelling) mouth, the stone (I am citing items consecutively from verse 3675), the coal, the forge, the nobles, the cough, the knocking again, the haunch bone, the flatulence, bread and ale, the cry of 'out' and 'harrow', the neighbors, the carpenter's arm, the gaping and staring, the carpenter's madness – are all prepared for beforehand. The breathtaking effect of the poem's climax surely owes much to this process. The focal image – the flood, the carpenter in his tub, the axe and cord – are suddenly brought to our conscious attention, not from nowhere (with an effect of mere surprise and chance), but from the semi-conscious storage of previous acceptance, unanticipated, perhaps, but inevitable. It is this solidity of detail, along with the characterization interlaced intimately with it, that gives the ingenious plotting its overpowering substantiality.[7]

Imagery, in the more restricted sense in which the term has here been used, contributes significantly to a number of these various facets which produce the acknowledged brilliance of the tale. As in his other fabliaux, Chaucer chooses formal figurative images which have ironic relevance beyond their immediate appropriateness, and these serve to reinforce the inevitability of the final scene and supplement the establishment of the essential natures of the four characters whose interaction with one another initiates the intrigue and directs it to its raucous denouement.

The frank animality of the tale, which stems not only from the

[6] Muscatine (note 4).
[7] *Ibid.*, pp. 225-6.

gross action throughout but also from the gaiety of its enactment, is substantiated by numerous similes comparing the characters to a wide variety of birds and beasts. As in the *Reeve's Tale*, Chaucer here uses figurative impressions to verify what the participants' deeds are to reveal. Alisoun is described as a weasel (3234), a wether (3249), a' swallow (3258), a kid (3260), a calf (3260), a colt (3263, 3282), a mouse (3346), and a bird (3699, 3726, 3805); Nicholas facetiously speaks of the old carpenter swimming as merrily as a duck after a drake (3576); Absolon is compared to a goose (3317), a cat (3347), a nightingale (3377), and an ape (3389), and he likens himself to a lamb (3704) and a turtle dove (3706). Only Nicholas is exempt from such direct figurative comparisons, yet he is a primary exponent of uncomplicated sensuality. Chaucer instead brings him into the pattern by a more circuitous method which ironically emphasizes the futility of Absolon's "love-longynge". As the narrator describes the parish clerk ogling Alisoun in church, he states:

> I dar wel seyn, if she hadde been a mous,
> And he a cat, he wolde hire hente anon.
>
> (3346-7)

Absolon, as it turns out, is in truth no cat: he lacks both feline secretiveness and preying skill. Nicholas, however, is directly linked to a literal cat whose entrance to his room is a hole "ful lowe upon a bord" (3440), and it is he who seizes Alisoun for precisely the intentions attributed to Absolon:

> And prively he *caughte* hire by the queynte,
> And seyde, "Ywis, but if ich have my wille,
> For deerne love of thee, lemman, I spille."
> And heeld hire harde by the haunchebones ...
>
> (3276-9)

Moreover, the verbs which Chaucer later uses to describe the two descending from the kneading tubs re-invoke the image of the cat and mouse, even though the latter is this time only too willing to be caught:

> Doun of the laddre *stalketh* Nicholay,
> And Alisoun *ful softe adoun she spedde*;
>
> (3648-9)

Significantly, Alisoun receives the bulk of the animal similes, most of which appear in her initial portrait. The artistry of this *effictio*, which succeeds in depicting all the appeal and unaffected loveliness of this "wenche" even as it ironically prescribes her essential limitations, has been frequently discussed.[8] Her youth, freshness, and vitality emerge through figurative comparisons. She resembles not only frisky young animals – the kid, the calf, and the colt – but also MORNING milk, a NEW "pere-jonette" tree, a NEW-FORGED noble, and a "prymerole", the flower of early spring. Simultaneously, she radiates a sensuous ripeness compounded from her likeness to a hoard of apples laid in hay, to drinks brewed from honey, to soft unclipped wool, and to the black sloe-plum. Because almost all of the images applied to her are taken from country life, she seems essentially a creature of nature, impelled by the innate, instinctive force that directs all living things toward fertility and fruition. Her uncomplicated sexuality needs only the proper mate so that it may fulfill its limited but natural animal function; yet, she has wed, in violation of the harmony of nature, an old man who can match her youthful vitality with the mere desperate lechery of approaching impotence. As Chaucer says:

> She was a prymerole, a piggesnye,
> For any lord to leggen in his bedde,
> Or yet for any good yeman to wedde.
>
> (3268-70)

In employing imagery to so characterize Alisoun, and in placing her portrait after the initial descriptions of the two men in her household – one old and jealous, the other young and "hende" [9] – Chaucer forecasts the intrigue which must inevitably ensue. Moreover, he may have selected two of the animal similes for a more specific ironic foreshadowing of the precise form of the

---

[8] See, for example: Lowes (note 2), pp. 218-19; Speirs, *Chaucer the Maker*, pp. 127-9; Muscatine (note 4), pp. 229-30; E. T. Donaldson, "Idiom of Popular Poetry in the *Miller's Tale*", *English Institute Essays, 1950* (New York, 1951), pp. 129-34.

[9] For excellent discussion of the ironic way in which this epithet shifts its meaning, see: Donaldson (note 8), pp. 122-5; Paul E. Beichner, "Chaucer's Hende Nicholas", *Mediaeval Studies*, XIV (1952), 151-3.

intrigue. If he is again playing with the pseudo-natural history of the bestiaries (and the frequent pertinence of their lore makes this seem at least possible), Alisoun's body "gent and small" as "any wezele" is more than an original fresh image [10] descriptive of both her physical appearance and her inner nature. It is an amusing anticipation of her activities on the ill-fated night yet to come, for the weasel, so say the bestiaries, moves with subtle cunning from one part of the house to another so that it lies each night in a different lair.[11] Even more ironically explicit is the comparison to the swallow. Not only is this bird symbolic of inconstancy,[12] but it is also popularly believed to leave the nest "when this will not stick to the roof-ridge and is going to tumble down".[13] Alisoun, of course, does something very similar to this, even though it is actually her husband's "nest" that tumbles and even though the fore-sight attributed to the swallow is hardly her motive.

Chaucer also seems to provide, through the consistency of his comparisons of Alisoun to things of nature, an explanation for her final position within the theme of self-deception which the tale develops. The much-discussed poetic justice meted out in the final scene explodes the pretensions of the three men involved. John is punished both for his lust which has led him to assume that he can possess Alisoun and for his pride in an ignorant "bileve" which he assumes to surpass intelligence and learning, Nicholas for his self-esteem of a secretive cleverness which he assumes can manipulate all circumstances to his own advantage, Absolon for his ridiculous delusions that he is an effective lover, courtly or otherwise. Alisoun, however, is spared the direct, physical retribution exacted from the other offenders. Because she has none of the pretentiousness variously exhibited by her suitors, because she has merely behaved in accord with the nature established for her through the comparisons to animal life and

[10] Lowes (note 2), p. 219.
[11] White, *The Bestiary*, p. 92.
[12] Droulers, *Dictionnaire*, p. 99.
[13] White (note 11), p. 147. The pertinence of this bit of lore has been noted previously by James R. Kreuzer, "The Swallow in Chaucer's 'Miller's Tale' ", *Modern Language Notes*, LXXIII (1958), 81.

nature's productivity, she is less culpable than the other three. Yet, although she is not guilty of self-deception, she is as much involved in the violation of moral order as they, and for this offense she too pays a penalty. In something of a Boethian sense,[14] her nature is her punishment. Because the circumstances of her marriage make acceptable fulfillment of her nature impossible, she can only endure an unsatisfying marital relationship or turn to adultery, and this solution may prove equally impossible in the future, once the old carpenter's jealous suspicions have been verified by the false Deluge.

Thus, the figurative comparisons applied to Alisoun not only define her essential nature but also ironically foreshadow her actions and prescribe her dubious position within the moral order underlying the tale.

The formal images in the initial sketches of Nicholas and Absolon also define character, and they have an ironic inter-relationship which emphasizes the potentialities of the two as lovers for the concupiscible Alisoun. As E. T. Donaldson has pointed out, Chaucer describes his parish clerk in the cliches which were customarily lavished upon medieval heroines,[15] there-by reinforcing the effeminateness suggested by his high-pitched voice ("he song som tyme a loud quynyble", 3332), his over-fastidious concern for his appearance, his obvious pleasure in sweet artificial smells, and his repugnance for their opposite. In

---

[14] In Book IV of *The Consolation of Philosophy*, when Boethius is instructed in the nature of good and evil, reward and punishment, Lady Philosophy asserts that just as good provides its own reward happiness, so evil is its own punishment: "... cum ipsum bonum beatitudo sit, bonos omnes eo ipso quod boni sint fieri beatos liquet. Sed qui beati sint deos esse conuenit. Est igitur praemium bonorum quod nullus deterat dies, nullius minuat potestas, nullius fuscet improbitas, deos fieri. Quae cum ita sint, de malorum quoque inseparabili poena dubitare sapiens nequeat. Nam cum bonum malumque item poenae atque praemium aduersa fronte dissideant, quae in boni praemio uidemus accedere eadem necesse est in mali poena contraria parte repondeant. Sicut igitur probis probitas ipsa fit praemium, ita improbis nequitia ipsa supplicium est. Iam uero quisquis afficitur poena, malo se affectum esse non dubitat."

Although "evil" is perhaps too strong a word for Alisoun's instinctive lustiness, her nature, diverted from its proper scope, does seem to provide precisely the sort of punishment which Philosophy describes.

[15] Donaldson (note 8), pp. 127-9.

addition to the red "rode", "greye eyes", and surplice "whit as is
the blosme upon the rys" noted by Professor Donaldson, Absolon's hair, like that of countless beautiful medieval women,
shines like gold,[16] and it spreads out large and broad "as a fanne",
an implement also suggestively feminine.[17] In this catalogue of
ideal beauty, however, there is one discordant note. Eyes, for
Chaucer as for his contemporaries, are conventionally "greye as
glas",[18] but Absolon's are "greye as *goos*".[19] This interjection of a
rather ridiculous, ungainly fowl into the description of dandified
elegance heightens the subtle irony of the portrait: Absolon is
absurd as well as effeminate. It is possible, moreover, that
Chaucer had yet another ironic purpose in choosing this simile,
for according to the popular lore of the bestiaries, no animal is
so sensitive to the smell of man as is the goose.[20] Just as Absolon
seems to have been made a barber (3326) in anticipation of his
later ignominious encounter with a "berd", so the reference to the
goose may relate to his equally ignominious encounter with man's
most internal smell.

In contrast to Nicholas' assertive masculinity, "derne" though
it be, Absolon's attractiveness to Alisoun can be but nil. His
effeminateness and the artificiality of his entire provincial version of courtly love provide no complement for her completely
natural lustiness. It is Nicholas' direct, physical appeal that
matches her own uncomplicated sexuality: she is indeed one of
those "folk" who "wol ben wonnen" for "strokes" (he "thakked
hire aboute the lendes weel", 3304) rather than "for richesse" or
"for gentillesse" (3381-2). This fact is underscored by one of the

---

[16] Curry, *Ideal of Personal Beauty*, pp. 12-15.
[17] Paul E. Beichner, "Absolon's Hair", *Mediaeval Studies*, XII (1950),
222-33, demonstrates that in the Middle Ages the Biblical Absalom,
through allegorical exegesis and the *Ubi sunt* poems, had acquired the
reputation for an equally feminine beauty.
[18] Chaucer uses the cliche for the Prioress (*Gen. Pro.*, 152) and for
Symkin's daughter (*Reeve's T.*, 3974). See also: Curry (note 16), pp. 51-2.
[19] Curry (note 16), p. 52, states that he found no other use of the simile
"greye as goos" in his investigations of romances, chronicles, and legends
of the thirteenth, fourteenth, and fifteenth centuries. Chaucer elsewere
uses the goose in the pejorative sense here suggested: *Merch. T.* 2275;
Troilus III, 584.
[20] White (note 11), p. 152.

similes used in the initial portrait of the clerk. Nicholas, we are told, is "as sweete as is the roote/ Of lycorys, or any cetewale" (3206-7). Ironically some four hundred lines later, we find Absolon chewing "greyn and *lycorys,*/ To smellen sweete" (3690-1).[21] What for Nicholas is a metaphoric description of real physical charm becomes for Absolon an artificial means of attaining what his supersensitive nose suggests will be effective physical appeal.

Equally ironic is the other figurative comparison in Nicholas' portrait:

> Of deerne love he koude and of solas;
> And therto he was sleight and ful privee,
> And *lyk a mayden meke for to see.*
>
> (3200-2)

To keep his strictly masculine activities secret, he assumes a feminine meekness, but this pose is strictly "for to see", a mask for his real nature. Absolon's exterior flamboyance is likewise a mask, designed to make him attractive to the opposite sex, but it unfortunately reveals a maidenliness discordant to his purpose. This same inadequacy is brilliantly climaxed in the imagery which he chooses for his love plea to Alisoun. He actually compares himself to a "mayde", a lamb, and a turtle-dove, the bird traditionally associated with the fidelity of women. His obsession for smells also recurs here as he calls Alisoun "hony-comb" and "my sweete cynamome", and, of course, his whole plea exposes the ridiculous inadequacy of his attempt to be a courtly lover. Particularly inept is his simile, "I moorne as dooth a lamb after the tete" (3704), a phrase loaded with devastating ramifications, unconscious in both the unwitting and the Freudian sense.

The initial description of John, the carpenter, contains only two figurative expressions, but both of them ironically foreshadow his ridiculous fate. He has, we are told, "fallen in the snare" of marrying a young wife when he is old:

---

[21] This detail has been noted by Earle Birney, "The Inhibited and the Uninhibited: Ironic Structure in the 'Miller's Tale' ", *Neophilologus*, XLIV (1960), 335.

He knew nat Catoun, for his wit was rude,
That bad man sholde wedde his simylitude.
Men sholde wedden after hire estaat,
For youthe and elde is often at debaat.
But *sith that he was fallen in the snare,*
He moste endure, as oother folk, his care.

(3227-32)

Moreover, because he is jealous and afraid of becoming a cuckold,
he holds his wife "narwe in cage" (3224). This seemingly innocuous expression for matrimonial watchfulness is charged with
ironic significance, for John's suspicions are well-founded, and
the guard which he keeps upon Alisoun is to lead to a circum-
vention in which he himself will be actually held "narwe" in a
cage-like contraption suspended from the rafters of his house.
Nicholas' craftiness turns the old man's metaphoric cage into a
literal one which, because it confines the wrong bird, facilitates
rather than prevents what the husband fears.

Similarly, the first "snare" mentioned early in the tale merely
anticipates a second in which John is to fall literally, and Chaucer
keeps the notion running throughout the intervening period by
repeated mentions of the key verb. After Nicholas has devised his
plan and locked himself in his chamber, he refuses to answer
Alisoun's calls no matter what "thyng that myghte *falle*" (3418),
thereby laying the groundwork for the plan destined to end in a
climactic fall which his own cleverness can in no way anticipate.
Then, upon hearing that Nicholas seems to be in a trance, John
immediately assumes that the clerk has lost his senses. He asserts:

This man is *falle,* with his astromye,
Into some *woodnesse* or in som *agonye.*

(3451-2)

And he goes on to discredit intellectual curiosity and recount an
anecdote about another clerk:

Men sholde nat knowe of Goddes pryvetee.
Ye, blessed be alwey a lewed man
That noght but oonly his bileve kan!
So ferde another clerk with astromye;
He walked in the feeldes, for to prye
Upon the sterres, what ther sholde bifalle,
Til he was in a marle-pit *yfalle* . . .   (3254-60)

Ironically, because Nicholas so manipulates his landlord's "bileve" [22] that John accepts the clerk's astronomical predictions of an event that is "Goddes pryvetee", John himself is to undergo the very same sort of accident which he here derides. In fact, in the final scene, he unintentionally reenacts precisely what he has said about Nicholas: he falls "into" the "agonye" of a broken arm and the "woodnesse" of being unanimously regarded mad:

> For what so that this carpenter answerde,
> It was for noght, no man his reson herde.
> With othes grete he was so sworn adoun
> That *he was holde wood* in al the toun ...
>
> (3843-6)

Because of this judgment, moreover, he can but "endure" in this second "snare" as in the one initially mentioned.

As Chaucer brings this theme of falling nearer to the final scene, he gradually shifts the meaning of the verb away from its original metaphoric sense and directs it step by step toward its literal culmination. The physical reality which the unnamed clerk's descent into the marle-pit introduces is transferred to John himself in the last of these ironic foreshadowings. As soon as he hears of the coming deluge, twice as great as "Noes flood", he cries out: "Allas, my wyf!/ And shal she drenche?" Then, 'for sorwe of this he fil almoost adoun" (3522-4). The qualifying "almost" is removed two hundred and ninety lines later. As soon as he hears Nicholas cry out "Help! water! water! help, for Goddes herte" (3815) and assumes that this announces the predicted flood, John follows the plan which is supposed to save the three from drowning, smites the cord "atwo", and crashes to the floor below.

Thus, an ironic image, introduced at the beginning of the tale, becomes the focus for use of the rhetorical figure *traductio*, and this reshaping of the key word through reiteration contributes to the sense of utter inevitability which Chaucer manages to create for the highly improbable climax. An inexorable though comic

---

[22]   John J. O'Connor, "The Astrological Background of the *Miller's Tale*", *Speculum*, XXXI (1956), 120-5, traces the tradition that Noah was a skillful astrologer who foresaw the Flood through study of the stars as well as being devinely forewarned, and he points out how Nicholas links revelation with his astrology in the report made to the credulous carpenter.

fate scourges with all the efficiency of its tragic counterpart because the poet has coalesced in his final moment not only literal
details and aspects of character previously developed but also
ironic imagery. Indeed, the whole headlong train of retribution is
set in motion by a shockingly graphic image which functions with
double significance of the levels of gross reality and metaphoric
aptness. Nicholas' hubristic insult, "As greet as it had been a
thonder-dent" (3807), not only excoriates Absolon and heralds
its perpetrator's own branding but also, like its atmospheric
counterpart, immediately precedes the deluge which, though it
exists only in the carpenter's mind, serves to drown John in a
flood of ridicule.

X

CONCLUSION

The suggestion was made at the outset of this study that Chaucer had developed a definitive technique for the handling of imagery within his fabliaux – a technique in which figurative comparisons are given ironic ramification which extends their meanings beyond the immediate points of reference and causes them to function organically within the aesthetic whole of the narrative. Upon the basis of the analyses presented in the preceding chapters, it is now possible to define more precisely the nature and significance of this technique.

In all of the tales here examined, Chaucer manipulates his formal rhetorical figures so that they interact ironically with some other aspect of the narrative. The irony may result from the relationship of the imagery to specific details appearing elsewhere in the story – as is most notably the case in the *Reeve's Tale*, the *Shipman's Tale*, and the *Merchant's Tale* – or it may emerge from the relevance of the figures of speech to the progress of the action – as in the *Friar's Tale*, the *Summoner's Tale*, and the *Miller's Tale*.

Chaucer's favorite use for such figurative comparisons is to provide an ironic foreshadowing of events yet to come: the old carpenter's falling into a snare, the summoner's dual role as hunter and heedless prey, the begging friar's unwittingly apt lecture, Symkin's "piled" skull and peacock qualities. The most elaborate example of this usage, of course, appears in the *Merchant's Tale*, where the final scene literally and ironically embodies the extensive paradise-hell theme previously developed. Equally consistent is the poet's inclusion of figurative comparisons which furnish ironic commentary upon various traits exhibited by individual characters. These qualities are always discernible in the characters' speech and actions, but Chaucer uses the relevant imagery to specify and emphasize what is of essential importance in their natures: the merchant's inadequate imitation of moral virtue, Alisoun's natural lustiness, January's spiritual rationalization, the friar's predatoriness, the animalism of the characters in the *Reeve's Tale*.

In fact, Chaucer never depends upon imagery alone to produce a desired result; instead, he consistently makes the irony achieved through imagery verify or reinforce effects which he is simultaneously creating through the more readily apparent elements of plot and characterization. Thus, the paradoxical relationships between the devil and the summoner, the merchant and his friend Daun John, Nicholas and Absolon – all of which are prescribed explicitly by ironic interplay of imagery – are also evident in the actions of the respective pairs. Likewise, the ironic imagery which specifically links cause with humiliating result in the *Reeve's Tale* and the *Summoner's Tale* merely sharpens and spices what the plot developments also illustrate. In both of these tales the structural relationship between the two major scenes is pointed out not only by the ironic interaction of imagery in one scene with literal detail in the other, but also by similar interplay of other devices – proverb, fable, and dialogue in the *Reeve's Tale*; pun, proverb, and exemplum in the *Summoner's Tale*. In like manner, the ironic imagery which culminates in the raucous climax of the *Miller's Tale* parallels an equal coalescence of previously mentioned concrete details and peculiarities of character.

In each tale the extended significance given to the various rhetorical figures tightens the unity of the artistic whole, and it contributes importantly to the ultimate meaning of the action. Chaucer's comic irony in these narratives consistently serves an essentially moral purpose: gross deviations from basic moral standards bring about their own deserved punishment, and thus the inherent infirmity in the aberration is indirectly revealed. Chaucer's technique with imagery underscores, clarifies, and deepens the significance of this irony. Through added illustration, it insists upon the basic importance of the irony to the underlying moral intention even though it is simultaneously providing delightfully amusing references. In the *Shipman's Tale* and the *Merchant's Tale*, where the offenders guilty of spiritual blindness remain equally blind to events which should be their punishment, Chaucer uses imagery to set up within the tale itself the moral and spiritual standard against which the characters' inadequacies become painfully obvious. In this process, as with the other functions achieved by his technique, Chaucer does not rely upon imagery alone but augments the solid religious framework with narrative detail, allusion, and scraps of dialogue.[1] One recent critic has said that "the close interrelationship between the ironist and the moralist in Chaucer is seldom underscored".[2] The role which imagery plays in that interrelationship surely deserves a consideration which has heretofore been neglected.

The complexity and significance of this whole technique, however, is never apparent on the surface of Chaucer's verse. His individual metaphors and similes are deceptively simple and lucid, and they always offer some sort of immediate sensory impression connected with their direct point of reference. This immediate impression may be vividly effective, but because Chaucer so frequently uses commonplace comparisons (proud as a peacock, still as a stone, mad as a hare), the response is often only vaguely sensory, the aptness of the juxtaposition being already established by long familiarity. In choosing these images, Chaucer is primarily concerned with their ironic correspondence to other parts of the narrative, although he always gives at least token attention to their sensory or descriptive quality. Thus, he asks that his readers respond INTELLECTUALLY to his imagery – or

---

[1] There is a similar background of religious reference in the *Miller's Tale*, which Paul N. Siegel has discussed in "Comic Irony in the *Miller's Tale*", *Boston University Studies in English*, IV (1960), 114-20, and about which R. E. Kaske has conjectured in "The 'Canticum Canticorum' in the 'Miller's Tale' ", *Studies in Philology*, LIX (1962), 479-500. In this instance, however, Chaucer does not use imagery to give added weight to what Mr. Siegel calls the "backdrop of the eternally significant".

[2] C. N. Stavrou, "Some Implications of Chaucer's Irony", *South Atlantic Quarterly*, LVI (1957), 455.

perhaps one should say that he at least provides them with ample opportunities to do so – and this process is not simple at all. If the subtlety of the imagery remains unnoted, however, the tale suffers merely in depth of effect rather than nature of effect since, as noted above, the imagery always functions as counterpart to meanings and relationships also developed by plot, character, and narrative detail.

The consistency with which Chaucer uses imagery in this way within the tales here considered suggests that the process is deliberate, conscious artistry. The perfection of the single ironic pattern found in the *Friar's Tale*, which contains no figurative rhetorical devices that do not contribute to the paradoxical hunter-prey image, can hardly be happy accident, and although the other tales do include occasional similes which seem relevant only in their immediate contexts, the number is amazingly few.[3] The similarity from tale to tale in the functions performed by the ironic imagery also argues for a conscious technique, however unwilling those modern theorists who favor a subconscious origin for imagery may be to admit the possibility.

From the writers of rhetorical-poetic treatises, Chaucer would have learned above all that the use of rhetorical figures is a deliberate process – in fact, conscious use of figures is the major burden of their song – and if his familiarity with these medieval theorists was as extensive as his references to them and his use of their formulae would suggest, he could not fail to consider as recognized poetic devices the figures which he uses to create his peculiar kind of imagery. Chaucer did not, however, derive his technique from their precepts any more than he found a suggestion for it in the sources from which he drew his plots. Indeed, the purposes for which he employs the *translatio, similitudo, imago, effictio,* and *demonstratio* suggest that he saw only too

---

[3] In terms of my own analysis, the *Shipman's Tale*, like the *Friar's Tale*, contains no figurative comparisons which do not have extended ironic relevance. The *Reeve's Tale* has one figure which seems to function merely by surface appropriateness, the *Merchant's Tale* five, the *Summoner's Tale* four. The *Miller's Tale* includes eleven, but even so the narrative demonstrates the presence of the technique far more frequently than it does its absence.

clearly the limitations of medieval poetic theory. In direct violation of the precepts, he uses rhetorical figures (and not only those
connected with imagery) for the comic and the overtly "low".
He does not equate aesthetic superiority to a social and moral
hierarchy of "worthiness", as Geoffrey of Vinsauf seems to do
– or perhaps it would be more accurate to say that his insight
into human nature has allowed him to realize that the "low", the
comic, may be so treated that it achieves a "worthiness" of its
own, the more effective for its unexpectedness. Moreover, his
technique of choosing images for their ironic relevance to other
portions of the narrative defies the theorists' concept of form and
thought as separable elements. With Chaucer, the form of these
images is the thought, and the pleasing surface appropriateness so
strongly recommended by Geoffrey is often merely secondary. As
suggested previously, his technique also reveals a unique concern
for organic wholeness. Although both Geoffrey and Matthew of
Vendôme consider this concept, they fail to explain or even to
attempt to explain how their rhetorical figures may relate to the
whole except by amplifying or abbreviating its size. Chaucer,
however, so interweaves his rhetorical images with the progress
and the purpose of the narrative that they actually denote the
relationship of various parts to the whole. Just as he twists specific conventional images, commonplace comparisons, and well-
known proverbs to suit his own unique intentions, just as he
vivifies the prosaic moral exemplum with dramatic conflict of
character, just as he transforms the vulgar fabliau into covert
moral exemplum, so he employs the conventions of the rhetoricians for purposes which they obviously had never envisioned. On
every level, he transcends the traditional even as he adheres to its
basic forms.

   One final implication of Chaucer's technique for creating irony
through imagery must be mentioned. There can be no doubt that
the poet lavished some of his most careful artistry upon these
tales for which he overtly apologizes. In the Miller's Prologue he
prays that "every gentil wight" will not think that he repeats these
fabliaux for "yvel entente"; he must record what he heard or else
"falsen" his materials:

And therfore, whoso list it nat yheere,
Turne over the leef and chese another tale;
For he shal fynde ynowe, grete and smale,
Of storial thyng that toucheth gentillesse,
And eek moralitee and hoolynesse.
Blameth nat me if that ye chese amys.
The Millere is a cherl, ye knowe wel this;
So was the Reve, and othere manye mo,
And harlotrie they tolden bothe two.
Avyseth yow, and put me out of blame;
And eek men shal nat maken ernest of game.

                                        (3176-86)

The ironic facetiousness of the poet's excusing himself for the
truthful repeating of what was said by fictitious characters of his
own creation is obvious. Is this passage, then, yet another example of Chaucer's indirect way of insinuating his real intentions? It
is true that if we regard the tales as dramatic monologues emerging
from their respective tellers, then the stories are "harlotrie". For
the Miller, the Shipman, and all the other "cherls" who ostensibly
narrate these tales, neither the moral implications nor the subtlety
of the imagery is feasible. But in his apology Chaucer subtly
points out the double standard of his narratives: on one level they
are fabliaux told by the respective pilgrims, and for this purpose
they are given a wealth of dramatic verisimilitude; on another
level they are the complexly artistic creations of the poet who
could both see and embody "ernest" in "game". When Chaucer
says "men shal nat maken ernest of game", is not this his ironic
way of stating that these tales contain more than first meets the
eye? Why should this statement be taken at face value, as some
critics have done, when nothing else in his presentation of himself in the *Canterbury Tales* can be? Just as his comments about
the "cherls' " words reveal the poet behind his characters, so this
negative injunction points the way to what Chaucer hopes his
audience, his readers, will perceive. The very process of per-
ceiving the depth of what these tales offer and the careful artistry
which establishes their significance requires close familiarity with
the tales, of course. Chaucer obviously hoped that his poetry
would be read again and again, either aloud or as he himself

poured over "olde bokes",[4] and, with a unique perception, aesthetic and moral and human, he labored to make these narratives merit such attention. By satisfying his own sensibilities, he might elevate the "low" to the "worthy". Yet, if his subtleties were overlooked, if his fabliaux were appreciated merely for what is apparent on the surface, he had already provided the proper response:

> Blameth nat *me* if that ye chese amys!

---

[4] The amusing rebuke to Adam, the scrivener, for the errors he makes in copying surely indicates Chaucer's desire for more than a transitory presentation of his works at court.

BIBLIOGRAPHY OF WORKS CITED

Adams, John F., "The Structure of Irony in *The Summoner's Tale*", *Essays in Criticism*, XII (1962), 126-32.

Armstrong, Edward A., *Shakespeare's Imagination* (London, 1946).

Atkins, J. W. H., *English Literary Criticism: The Medieval Phase* (Cambridge, 1943).

Augustine, Aurelius, St., *De doctrina christiana*, IV, ed. Sister Thérèse Sullivan (Washington, D.C., 1930).

Baldwin, Charles Sears, "Cicero on Parnassus", *PMLA*, XLII (1927), 106-12.

——, *Medieval Rhetoric and Poetic* (New York, 1928).

Baldwin, Ralph, "The Unity of the Canterbury Tales", *Anglistica*, V (Copenhagen, 1955).

Baugh, Albert C., "The Merchant's Tale", *Modern Philology*, XXXV (1937), 15-26.

Baum, Paull F., "Chaucer's Nautical Metaphors", *South Atlantic Quarterly*, XLIX (1950), 67-73.

——, "Chaucer's Puns", *PMLA*, LXXI (1956), 225-46.

Beichner, Paul E., "Absolon's Hair", *Mediaeval Studies*, XII (1950), 222-33.

——, "Chaucer's Hende Nicholas", *Mediaeval Studies*, XIV (1952), 151-3.

——, "Non Alleluia Ructare", *Mediaeval Studies*, XVIII (1956), 135-44.

Bennett, H. S., "Medieval Literature and the Modern Reader", *Essays and Studies*, XXXI (1945), 7-18.

Birney, Earle, " 'After His Ymage': the Central Ironies of the 'Friar's Tale' ", *Mediaeval Studies*, XXI (1959), 17-35.

——, "English Irony Before Chaucer", *University of Toronto Quarterly*, VI (1937), 538-57.

——, "Structural Irony within the Summoner's Tale", *Anglia*, LXXVIII (1960), 204-18.

——, "The Beginnings of Chaucer's Irony", *PMLA*, LIV (1939), 637-55.

——, "The Inhibited and the Uninhibited: Ironic Structure in the 'Miller's Tale' ", *Neophilologus*, XLIV (1960), 333-7.

Bloomfield, Morton W., *The Seven Deadly Sins* (East Lansing, 1952).

Boethius, *The Theological Tractates and the Consolation of Philosophy* (Loeb Classical Library, New York, 1918).

Bonjour, Adrien, "Aspects of Chaucer's Irony in 'The Friar's Tale'", *Essays in Criticism*, XI (1961), 121-7.

Bowden, Muriel, *A Commentary on the General Prologue to the Canterbury Tales* (New York, 1957).

Bronson, Bertrand H., "Afterthoughts on the Merchant's Tale", *Studies in Philology*, LVIII (1961), 583-96.

——, "*The Book of the Duchess* Re-opened", *PMLA*, LXVII (1952), 863-81.

Brown, Carleton, "The Evolution of the Canterbury 'Marriage Group'", *PMLA*, XLVIII (1933), 1041-59.

Brown, Stephen J., *The World of Imagery* (London, 1927).

Bryan, William Frank, and Germaine Dempster, *Sources and Analogues of Chaucer's Canterbury Tales* (Chicago, 1941).

Burrow, J. A., "Irony in the Merchant's Tale", *Anglia*, LXXV (1957), 199-208.

Caldwell, Robert A., "Chaucer's Taillyinge Ynough, Canterbury Tales, B² 1624", *Modern Language Notes*, LV (1940), 262-5.

Chapman, R. W., "*The Shipman's Tale* Was Meant for the Shipman", *Modern Language Notes*, LXXI (1956), 4-5.

Chaucer, Geoffrey, *The Works of Geoffrey Chaucer*, ed. F. N. Robinson, 2nd ed. (Cambridge, 1957).

——, *The Works of Geoffrey Chaucer*, ed. W. W. Skeat, 6 vols. (Oxford, 1894-1900).

(Cicero), *Ad C. Herennium*, ed. Harry Caplan (Loeb Classical Library, Cambridge, 1954).

Clemen, Wolfgang, *The Development of Shakespeare's Imagery* (Cambridge, 1951).

Coghill, Nevill, *The Poet Chaucer* (Oxford, 1949).

Cunningham, J. V., "The Literary Form of the Prologue to the *Canterbury Tales*", *Modern Philology*, XLIX (1952), 172-81.

Curry, Walter Clyde, "Chaucer's Reeve and Miller", *PMLA*, XXXV (1920), 189-209.

——, *The Middle English Ideal of Personal Beauty; as Found in the Metrical Romances, Chronicles, and Legends of the XIII, XIV, and XV Centuries* (Baltimore, 1916).

Curtius, Ernst R., *European Literature and the Latin Middle Ages*, trans. Willard R. Trask (New York, 1953).

Danby, John F., "Eighteen lines of Chaucer's 'Prologue'", *Critical Quarterly*, II (1960), 28-32.

Day Lewis, Cecil, *The Poetic Image* (New York, 1948).

Dempster, Germaine, *Dramatic Irony in Chaucer, Stanford University Publications in Language and Literature*, IV, no. 3 (1932).

——, "The 'Merchant's Tale'", *Modern Philology*, XXXIV (1936), 133-54.

Deschamps, Eustache, *Œuvres Complètes d'Eustache Deschamps*, ed. Gaston Raynaud, Société des Anciens Textes Français, IX (Paris, 1894).

Donaldson, E. T., ed., *Chaucer's Poetry* (New York, 1958).

——, "Idiom of Popular Poetry in the *Miller's Tale*", *English Institute Essays, 1950* (New York, 1951), pp. 116-40.

Donovan, Mortimer J., "The Image of Pluto and Proserpine in the *Merchant's Tale*", *Philological Quarterly*, XXXVI (1957), 49-60.

Droulers, Eug., *Dictionnaire des Attributs, Allégories, Emblèmes et Symboles* (Turnhout, Belgium, 1948).

Duncan, Edgar Hill, "Narrator's Points of View in the Portrait-sketches, Prologue to the *Canterbury Tales*", *Essays in Honor of Walter Clyde Curry* (Nashville, 1954), pp. 77-101.

Eliot, T. S., *Selected Essays, 1917-1932* (New York, 1932).

Evans, E. P., *Animal Symbolism in Ecclesiastical Architecture* (New York, 1906).

Everett, Dorothy, "Some Reflections on Chaucer's 'Art Poetical' ", *Essays on Middle English Literature* (Oxford, 1955).

Fansler, Dean S., *Chaucer and the Roman de la Rose* (New York, 1914).

Faral, Edmund, *Les Arts Poétiques du XIIe et XIIIe Siècle* (Paris, 1924).

Franc, Helen M., ed., *The Animal Kingdom, Illustrated Catalogue of an Exhibition of Manuscript Illuminations, Book Illustrations, Drawings, Cylinder Seals and Bindings* (New York, 1940-1).

French, Robert Dudley, *A Chaucer Handbook* (New York, 1947).

Garrett, Robert Max, "The Lay of Sir Gawayne and the Green Knight", *JEGP*, XXIV (1925), 125-34.

Godefroy, Frederic, *Dictionnaire de l'ancienne langue française*, 10 vols. (Paris, 1889).

Gordon, R. K., "Chaucer's Imagery", *Transactions of the Royal Society of Canada*, XXXIII, ser. 3, sec. 2 (1939), 81-90.

Hamilton, Marie Padgett, "Notes on Chaucer and the Rhetoricians", *PMLA*, XLVII (1932), 403-9.

Hankins, John Erskine, *Shakespeare's Derived Imagery* (Lawrence, 1953).

Harrison, Benjamin S., "Medieval Rhetoric in the *Book of the Duchess*", *PMLA*, XLIX (1934), 428-42.

Hart, Walter Morris, "The Reeve's Tale: A Comparative Study of Chaucer's Narrative Art", *PMLA*, XXIII (1908), 1-44.

Heilman, Robert B., *This Great Stage* (Baton Rouge, 1948).

Hinckley, Henry Barrett, "Chauceriana", *Modern Philology*, XVI (1918), 39.

Hoffman, Arthur W., "Chaucer's Prologue to Pilgrimage: The Two Voices", *ELH*, XXI (1954), 1-16.

Homann, Elizabeth Rudisill, "Kinesthetic Imagery in Chaucer" (Doctoral dissertation, University of California, Berkeley, 1948).

Huizinga, Johan, *The Waning of the Middle Ages* (London, 1924).

Hulbert, J. R., "Chaucer's Pilgrims", *PMLA*, LXIV (1949), 823-8.

——, "Sir Gawayn and the Grene Knyȝt", *Modern Philology*, XIII (1915), 433-62.

Hulme, T. E., *Speculations* (New York, 1924).

John of Garland, *Poetria*, ed. Giovanni Mari, *Romanische Forschungen*, XIII (1902), 883-965.

Jones, Claude, "Chaucer's Taillynge Ynough", *Modern Language Notes*, LII (1937), 570.

Jordan, Robert M., "The Non-dramatic Disunity of the *Merchant's Tale*", *PMLA*, LXXVIII (1963), 293-9.

Kaske, R. E., "The 'Canticum Canticorum' in the 'Miller's Tale' ", *Studies in Philology*, LIX (1962), 479-500.

Kellogg, Alfred L., "Susannah and the *Merchant's Tale*", *Speculum*, XXXV (1960), 275-9.

Klaeber, Friedrich, *Das Bild bei Chaucer* (Berlin, 1893).

Knight, G. Wilson, *The Crown of Life* (London, 1947).

——, *The Imperial Theme* (London, 1939).

——, *The Shakespearean Tempest* (London, 1932).

——, *The Wheel of Fire* (London, 1930).

Koeppel, Emil, "Chaucer und Albertanus Brixiensis", *Archiv*, LXXXVI (1891), 29-46.

Kökeritz, Helge, "Rhetorical Word-Play in Chaucer", *PMLA*, LXIX (1954), 937-52.

Kreuzer, James R., "The Swallow in Chaucer's 'Miller's Tale' ", *Modern Language Notes*, LXXIII (1958), 81.

Kurath, Hans, and Sherman M. Kuhn, eds., *Middle English Dictionary* (Part c.5. Ann Arbor, 1960).

Lawrence, William W., "Chaucer's *Shipman's Tale*", *Speculum*, XXXIII (1958), 56-68.

Legouis, Emile, *Geoffrey Chaucer* (Blond, 1910).

Lowes, John Livingston, "Chaucer and the *Miroir de Mariage*", *Modern Philology*, VIII (1910), 165-86.

——, *Geoffrey Chaucer* (Boston, 1934).

——, "Simple and Coy", *Anglia*, XXXIII (1910), 440-51.

Lucretius, *De Rerum Natura*, ed. Cyril Bailey, I (Oxford, 1947).

Lumiansky, R. M., *Of Sondry Folk* (Austin, 1955).

Makarewicz, Sister Mary Raynelda, *The Patristic Influence on Chaucer* (Doctoral dissertation, Catholic University, Washington, D.C., 1953).

Manly, John Matthews, *Chaucer and the Rhetoricians* (Warton Lecture on English Poetry, 17, Milford, 1926).

——, *Some New Light on Chaucer* (New York, 1926).

McGalliard, John C., "Chaucerian Comedy: The *Merchant's Tale*, Jonson and Molière", *Philological Quarterly*, XXV (1946), 343-70.

——, "Chaucer's *Merchant's Tale* and Deschamps' *Miroir de Mariage*", *Philological Quarterly*, XXV (1946), 193-220.

McKeon, Richard, "Rhetoric in the Middle Ages", *Speculum*, XVII (1942), 1-32.

Meech, Sanford Brown, *Design in Chaucer's Troilus* (Syracuse, 1959).

——, "Figurative Contrasts in Chaucer's *Troilus and Criseyde*", *English Institute Essays, 1950* (New York, 1951), pp. 57-88.

Mroczkowski, Przemyslaw, " 'The Friar's Tale' and its Pulpit Background", *English Studies Today*, 2nd series (1961), 107-20.

Murphy, James J., "Chaucer, Gower, and the English Rhetorical Tradition" (Doctoral dissertation, Stanford University, Stanford, 1956).

Murry, John Middleton, "Metaphor", *Countries of the Mind*, 2nd series (London, 1931).

Muscatine, Charles, *Chaucer and the French Tradition* (Los Angeles and Berkeley, 1957).

——, "Form, Texture and Meaning in Chaucer's *Knight's Tale*", *PMLA*, LXV (1950), 911-29.

Naunin, Traugott, *Der Einfluss der mittelalterlichen Rhetorik auf Chaucers Dichtung* (Bonn, 1929).

O'Connor, John J., "The Astrological Background of the *Miller's Tale*", *Speculum*, XXXI (1956), 120-5.

Olson, Paul A., "Chaucer's Merchant and January's 'Hevene in Erthe Heere' ", *ELH*, XXVIII (1961), 203-14.

Owen, Charles A., "Chaucer's *Canterbury Tales*: Aesthetic Design in the Stories of the First Day", *English Studies*, XXXV (1954), 49-56.

——, "The Crucial Passages in Five of the *Canterbury Tales*: A Study in Irony and Symbol", *JEGP*, LII (1953), 294-311.

Paetow, Louis John, *The Arts Course at Medieval Universities with Special Reference to Grammar and Rhetoric, University of Illinois Studies*, III, no. 7 (Urbana, 1910).

Payne, Robert O., *The Key of Remembrance: A Study of Chaucer's Poetics* (New Haven, 1963).

Pearsall, Derek A., "Rhetorical 'Descriptio' in Sir Gawain and the Green Knight", *Modern Language Review*, L (1955), 129-34.

Physiologus, trans. James Carlill, in *The Epic of the Beast* (London, 1924).

Physiologus: A Metrical Bestiary of Twelve Chapters by Bishop Theobald, trans. Alan Wood Rendell (London, 1928).

Pound, Ezra, *Instigations* (New York, 1920).

Pratt, Robert Armstrong, "The Classical Lamentations in the *Nun's Priest's Tale*", *Modern Language Notes*, LXIV (1949), 76-8.

Preston, Raymond, *Chaucer* (London, 1952).

Richards, I. A., *The Philosophy of Rhetoric* (London, 1936).

——, *Principles of Literary Criticism* (London, 1924).

Richardson, Janette, "An Ambiguous Reference in Chaucer's *Friar's Tale*", *Archiv*, CXCVIII (1962), 388-90.

Robertson, D. W., Jr., *A Preface to Chaucer: Studies in Medieval Perspectives* (Princeton, 1962).

——, "The Doctrine of Charity in Mediaeval Literary Gardens: A Topical Approach through Symbolism and Allegory", *Speculum*, XXVI (1951), 24-49.

——, "Why the Devil Wears Green", *Modern Language Notes*, LXIX (1954), 470-2.

Root, Robert Kilburn, *The Poetry of Chaucer* (New York, 1906).

Scudder, Vida, *Le Morte Darthur of Sir Thomas Malory and Its Sources* (New York, 1917).

Sedgewick, G. G., "The Structure of *The Merchant's Tale*", *University of Toronto Quarterly*, XVII (1948), 337-45.

Siegel, Paul N., "Comic Irony in the *Miller's Tale*", *Boston University Studies in English*, IV (1960), 114-20.

Silverman, Albert H., "Sex and Money in Chaucer's *Shipman's Tale*", *Philological Quarterly*, XXXII (1953), 329-36.

Sister Mary Immaculate, " 'Sixty' as a Conventional Number and Other Chauceriana", *Modern Language Quarterly*, II (1941), 59-66.

Skeat, W. W., *Early English Proverbs* (Oxford, 1910).

Speirs, John, *Chaucer the Maker* (London, 1951).

Spurgeon, Caroline, *Shakespeare's Imagery and What It Tells Us* (Cambridge, 1935).

Stauffer, Donald A., *Shakespeare's World of Images* (New York, 1949).

Stavrou, C. N., "Some Implications of Chaucer's Irony", *South Atlantic Quarterly*, LVI (1957), 454-61.

Steadman, John M., "The Prioress' Dogs and Benedictine Discipline", *Modern Philology*, LIV (1956), 1-6.

Stillwell, Gardiner, "Chaucer's 'Sad' Merchant", *Review of English Studies*, XX (1944), 1-18.

Tatlock, J. S. P., "Chaucer's *Merchant's Tale*", *Modern Philology*, XXXIII (1936), 367-81.

——, *The Development and Chronology of Chaucer's Works* (London, 1907).

——, "The Marriage Service in Chaucer's *Merchant's Tale*", *Modern Language Notes*, XXXII (1917), 373-4.

——, "Notes on Chaucer: The Canterbury Tales", *Modern Language Notes*, XXIX (1914), 144.

Taylor, Archer, "The Devil and the Advocate", *PMLA*, XXXVI (1921), 269-74.

Tillyard, E. M. W., *Poetry Direct and Oblique* (London, 1948).

Tornwall, William A., "Studies in Chaucer's Imagery" (Doctoral dissertation, Louisiana State University, Baton Rouge, 1956).

Tupper, Frederick, "The Bearings of the Shipman's Prologue", *JEGP*, XXXIII (1934), 352-72.

Utley, Francis Lee, *The Crooked Rib* (Columbus, 1944).

Vinaver, Eugene, ed., *The Works of Sir Thomas Malory*, I (Oxford, 1947).

Watson, Foster, *The English Grammar Schools to 1660: their Curriculum and Practice* (Cambridge, 1908).

Wellek, René, and Austin Warren, *Theory of Literature* (New York, 1942).

White, T. H., ed., *The Bestiary, A Book of Beasts* (London, 1954).

Whitesell, J. Edwin, "Chaucer's Lisping Friar", *Modern Language Notes*, LXXI (1956), 160-1.

Williams, Arnold, "Chaucer and the Friars", *Speculum*, XXVIII (1953), 499-513.

Woolf, Rosemary, "Chaucer as a Satirist in the General Prologue to the Canterbury Tales", *Critical Quarterly*, I (1959), 150-7.

Wright, Thomas, ed., *Anecdota Literaria* (London, 1841).

——, *Popular Treatises on Science Written during the Middle Ages* (London, 1841).

Young, Karl, "Chaucer and Geoffrey of Vinsauf", *Modern Philology*, XLI (1944), 172-82.

INDEX

STUDIES IN ENGLISH LITERATURE

29. ROBERT R. HODGES: *The Dual Heritage of Joseph Conrad.* 1967. 229 pp. Gld. 27.—

30. GEORGE R. LEVINE: *Henry Fielding and the Dry Mock: A Study of the Techniques of Irony in His Early Works.* 1967. 160 pp. Gld. 20.—

31. ERIC LAGUARDIA: *Nature Redeemed: The Imitation of Order in Three Renaissance Poems.* 1966. 180 pp. Gld. 21.50

32. RONALD EDGAR BARNES: *The Dramatic Comedy of William Somerset Maugham.* 1968. 180 pp. Gld. 21.—

33. F. PARVIN SHARPLESS: *The Literary Criticism of John Stuart Mill.* 1968. 250 pp. Gld. 28.—

34. ROBERT DONALD SPECTOR: *English Literary Periodicals and the Climate of Opinion during the Seven Year's War.* 1966. 408 pp. Gld. 43.—

35. BETTY J. LITTLETON: *"Clyomon and Clamydes": A Critical Edition.* 1968. 199 pp. Gld. 26.—

37. JOHN H. DORENKAMP: *"Beggar's Bush": A Critical Edition.* 1968. 200 pp. Gld. 25.—

38. JAMES H. CONOVER: *Thomas Dekker: An Analysis of Dramatic Structure.* 1969. 250 pp. Gld. 34.—

39. D. C. YELTON: *Mimesis and Metaphor: An Inquiry into the Genesis and Scope of Conrad's Symbolic Imagery.* 1968. 366 pp. Gld. 32.—

40. COBURN GUM: *The Aristophanic Comedies of Ben Jonson: A Comparative Study of Jonson and Aristophanes.* 1969. 207 pp. Gld. 30.—

41. SHEROD M. COOPER: *The Sonnets of Astrophel and Stella: A Stylistic Study.* 1968. 184 pp. Gld. 26.—

42. MARION TAYLOR: *A New Look at the Old Sources of Hamlet.* 1968. 79 pp. Gld. 15.—

43. CHARLES S. HENSLEY: *The Later Career of George Wither.* 1969. 156 pp. Gld. 24.—

44. JOHN POLLARD GUINN: *Shelley's Political Thought.* 1969. 134 pp. Gld. 18.—

45. GERALD E. ENSCOE: *Eros and the Romantics: Sexual Love as a Theme in Coleridge, Shelley and Keats.* 1968. Gld. 20.—

46. CHARLES J. LEES: *The Poetry of Walter Haddon.* 1967. 314 pp. Gld. 36.—

48. KENNETH B. NEWELL: *Structure in Four Novels by H. G. Wells.* 1968. 120 pp. Gld. 18.—

49. STANTON DE VOREN HOFFMAN: *Comedy and Form in the Fiction of Joseph Conrad.* 1969. 138 pp. Gld. 21.—

52. WILLIAM R. BRASHEAR: *The Living Will: A Study of Tennyson and Nineteenth-Century Subjectivism.* 1969. 178 pp. Gld. 30.—

54. ROBERT F. LEE: *Conrad's Colonialism.* 1969. 148 pp. Gld. 26.—

All volumes clothbound.

MOUTON · PUBLISHERS · THE HAGUE